The Church is a Gift – Assembly Required

Timothy R. Wood

The Church is a Gift – Assembly Required by Timothy R. Wood

Calvary Gospel Church

11150 Berry Road

Waldorf, MD 20603

www.calvarygospel.org

Unless otherwise noted, scriptures quoted are from the New King James Version of the Bible. Copyright © 1979, 1980, 1982 by Thomas Nelson Inc., publishers. Used by permission.

Scripture quotations marked KJV are from the King James Version of the Bible.

Publishing Consultant Services provided by Kelley Perry Enterprises

ISBN: 978-0692803912

ISBN-10: **0692803912**

Printed in the United States of America.

DEDICATION

I would like to dedicate this book to my four children, Joseph, Micah, Abigail and Alisa who enjoyed the privileges and endured the pain of growing up in a parsonage.

CONTENTS

INTRODUCTION

The local church has fallen on hard times. For many, the idea of church conjures up negative emotions because of churches that abuse. The answer is not to sever the body of Christ from its head because a decapitated Christ does not have impact on our world. Our resurrected and ascended Christ longs to be embodied in each community through the ministries of the local assembly.

Christ loves the church and gave Himself for her. If we love Christ, how can we not love what He loves? Loving Christ means that we love His church. Love means we express kind and appropriate behavior toward the beloved and how we treat the church is an important aspect of our passionate love for Christ.

The Bible is plain on how we treat the church. Yes, there are liberties we can take in forming church government, developing style, forming liturgy, shaping vision, sponsoring programs and choosing facilities. However, not every local church will look exactly alike! The Bible is the manual that provides for us a basic blueprint on how to construct a local church. There are some basic planks and parameters that make a church a true church. It is important that we "do church right." God always demands that we do His work His way!

At the conclusion of my seventh year as Senior Pastor to the great congregation of Calvary Gospel Church, we celebrated our 30 year anniversary, and it was then that I desired with great expectation to set forth God's vision for the next 30 years. I expressed my sincere hope that I will have that joy to serve the beautiful people of God and see that vision come to pass.

In January of 2015, I kicked off a Sunday morning series of sermons entitled "Calvary Gospel and the Next 30 years." This book contains some of the sermons that were delivered in the course of that year. Since these are sermons, they are formatted in a simple style that reflects the plain expressions that a public speaker needs to be effective. The terms are less technical and the sentences shorter than what would be used in the formal writing of a book.

Calvary Gospel enjoys distinctives that other churches will not embrace. We do not consider our format of worship superior to others, but we do seek to be biblical in theology and methods.

The objective of this book is to train the congregation of Calvary Gospel to enter into the vision that God ordained for our ministry. This book will be used for confirmation classes and new membership classes. The second objective of this book is to reach a larger audience and share Biblical principles on the development of local church ministry.

I trust the book will be received with joy and prove to be edifying to the Body of Christ

A SHOWING-UP CHURCH

Hebrews 10:19-27

Therefore, brethren, having boldness to enter the Holiest by the blood of Jesus, by a new and living way which He consecrated for us, through the veil, that is, His flesh, and having a High Priest over the house of God, let us draw near with a true heart in full assurance of faith, having our hearts sprinkled from an evil conscience and our bodies washed with pure water. Let us hold fast the confession of our hope without wavering, for He who promised is faithful. And let us consider one another in order to stir up love and good works, not forsaking the assembling of ourselves together, as is the manner of some, but exhorting one another, and so much the more as you see the Day approaching. For if we sin willfully after we have received the knowledge of the truth, there no longer remains a sacrifice for sins, but a certain fearful expectation of judgment, and fiery indignation which will devour the adversaries.

There is a serious problem plaguing American sanctuaries today—sagging church attendance. Many only come to church four times in their lives: when they are born to get christened, when they are in serious trouble and need prayer, when they get married and want a ceremony, and when they die and want to get buried. Just four times: hatch, patch, match, and dispatch. First time we throw water, second time we throw oil, third time we throw rice, and fourth time we throw dirt.

Church neglect is a grave concern. In Europe, only 6 percent of the population attends service on Sunday morning. In a country filled with huge, beautiful cathedrals where great crowds would once gather to celebrate the Lord's Day, it is slightly eerie that now only a few people are sprinkled throughout the massive buildings. I hope America does not follow this pattern, but it is seems to be the trend.

A *Newsweek* cover story published during the week of Easter 2012 stated the message simply: "Forget the church, follow Jesus." There are many who come into the church only to make a quick exit. They get baptized and become members, but as soon as something displeasing or unsatisfying occurs, they fade away from the church scene. I call these "Alka-Seltzer Christians": you dip them in water, they fizzle for a little while, and then they disappear.

The early Christian community perceived church absence as a serious problem. If a person willingly and deliberately developed a habit of missing church, it was assumed that this person was backsliding in their faith and falling victim to the temptations of the world. The writer of Hebrews expressed faithful church attendance as a serious matter: "Forsake not the assembly of yourselves together" (Hebrews 11:25). He precedes that exhortation by giving us three reasons why we need to show up.

Notice the repetitious phrase, **Let us.** (Verse 22) —"let us draw near." Verse 23 – "let us hold fast." Verse 24 –"let us consider." Since most sermons are supposed to have three points, this format provides us with an outline for a wonderful sermon. Let us take the three "let us" statements of the text and build our exhortation around them. Why *do* we show up to church?

We Show Up to Worship

"Let us draw near with a true heart in full assurance of faith, having our hearts sprinkled from an evil conscience and our bodies washed with pure water." — Hebrews 10:22

What is the #1 reason for gathering at church? To exalt Christ and to worship Him! We draw near to Christ in His Father's house so that we might penetrate His intimate presence, encounter His magnificent glory, and rejoice in who He is and what He does. Congregational gathering is all about Jesus. Revelation 1 pictures Him as the living Christ who walks among the "candlesticks," a biblical reference to the churches. He made this promise to His followers, "If two or three are gathered in My name, I am in the midst of them" (Matthew 18:20).

The church and Jesus Christ are not identical, but they are inseparable. The church is likened to three figures: body, bride, and building. As a body, the church members represent various parts of the body, each fulfilling their specific function, with Christ as the head. Not identical, but inseparable. Sever the head from the body, and big trouble will ensue.

As a bride, the church waits on her beloved groom, Jesus Christ, and she is united to Him as one flesh. There is a mystical union. Not identical, but inseparable.

As a building, the church is a superstructure built upon the foundation of Christ. Who can enjoy a foundation without the refuge of a building? And who would want to be in a building if it is not firmly placed on a foundation? Not identical, but inseparable.

It is grossly illogical and theologically heretical to say, "I love Jesus, but I don't like the church." Christ loves the church and gave Himself for her (Ephesians 5:25). To love Christ, we must love what He loves.

We attend church to be close to God and close to His people. Let *us*—plural— draw near. Drawing near to God is a group affair, and we can draw near because a new and living way has been consecrated for us. In the new covenant, the veil has been torn asunder, the obstacles have been removed, and the distance has been overcome. Through Christ, we have bold and confident access to God and all His resources.

At a key moment during the Civil War, President Lincoln reluctantly signed a no-furlough order. It broke his heart to keep the enlisted men of the Union from going home to see their loved ones, but their service in the battle was more important. One soldier had made his way to Washington, D.C. to see the President to request an exemption. He wanted a furlough to see his dying wife at home, but he was not allowed past the guards. He had no appointment, no access. He hung his head in sadness and left the White House. Outside he caught the eye of a ten year old boy.

When this boy saw the dejected soldier, he ran up to him: "What's the matter, sir?" he asked. The soldier replied, "My wife is dying, and I wanted a furlough so I could be with her, but they won't let me see the President." The little child said, "Is that so? Well, take my hand." They joined hands, and the small boy led this soldier up the stairs, past the guards, through the big doors, and right into the oval office. The President looked up from underneath a mound of paperwork and asked, "What is it, Tad?" Little Tad, the President's son, proceeded to introduce the soldier, and the soldier made his request. The request was granted, and the soldier was permitted to see his wife.

Without Christ, we had no access to the Father's majesty. Through God's Son, we now have access to the most Holy Place. What an honor and a privilege to gather together on Sunday mornings and draw near to God Himself!

We Show Up to Witness

"Let us hold fast the confession of our hope without wavering, for He who promised is faithful." – Hebrews 10:23

Former presidential candidate and New York Governor, Alfred Smith, told of the time when he was a member of the fishing party in New England. Smith is a very devout believer, and on Sunday morning he and a few of his fishing buddies rolled out of bed early to make their way to the local church. As they tiptoed past their snoring, sleeping mates, he heard one of the half- asleep men, who was cozied up under a heavy blanket, mutter, "Wouldn't it be awful if it turned out they were right?" Even unbelievers have their moments of doubt. The fact is, our church attendance and involvement is a huge witness to our community.

When you get up early on Sunday morning and put on your Sunday best, and when you pull your car out of the driveway with a big Bible lodged on the dashboard—what a testimony that is! Your neighbors know that you are making your way to church—they are peeking out the window, taking notice of your action! Faithful church attendance makes an impression on the community around you.

It's not easy going to church on Sunday morning. Most of us would love to sleep in, have breakfast in bed, watch the news report on TV, read the newspaper, laugh at the funny papers, get some gardening done, or go to the grocery store while it is empty to catch up on shopping. It's a hassle getting up, getting dressed, getting the kids ready, and getting to church. To add fuel to the fire, the devil will fight you—there is spiritual warfare every Sunday morning.

When I was growing up, we had what was called the "Sunday morning fight." Yes, we did have an official name for it. In reality, we were a very peaceful and loving family...just not on Sunday mornings.

Mom and Dad would fuss because he wanted to leave for church at 9:00 AM, but she wanted to leave at 9:30. I would hear them holler in the back bed room, "Ray, church doesn't start until 10:00. I don't want to sit there for thirty minutes. I'm not finished with my hair." Dad would respond, "Rosey, we are leaders, and we need to get there early. We need to talk to people. I hate getting there at the last minute." In the end, they would resolve to take two cars. My sister was always grumpy on Sunday morning because she hated Sunday School. "Do I have to sit in that scary basement and listen to Elder Tom read the Sunday School commentary for 45 minutes? This is child abuse." Jimmy was mad at me for eating all the cereal and grabbing the prize at the bottom of the box. Oh, Sunday morning was a circus.

Quite frankly, the devil doesn't want you to come to church on Sunday, especially not with praise on your lips and thanksgiving in your heart. Bob Evans is a much easier choice over Calvary Gospel Church. For many, my sermons are not as delicious as those pancakes and bacon.

I just made an emergency trip to Texas to help a family. I flew into Houston, drove over to Louisiana, and a few days later drove back to Texas to fly home. As I crossed the state line, I looked up and noticed a sign: "Welcome to Texas! Hope You're Hungry." There is a beef steak restaurant on every corner in Texas. In fact, to be in Texas and *not* be hungry is an insult to the State! Well, I want to put up a sign: "Welcome to Calvary Gospel... Hope You're Hungry!" We come to church because we need more than a hot biscuit on Sunday morning from IHOP. In addition to a physical appetite, we also hunger for the Word and thirst for the Spirit, so we come to church seeking God wholeheartedly.

Just as the following Psalms declare, we witness to the fact that only God can satisfy our spiritual appetites:

> ➤ *"One thing I have desired of the Lord, that will I seek: that I may dwell in the house of the Lord all the days of my life, to behold the beauty of the Lord, and to*

inquire in His temple." – Psalm 27:4

➤ *"As the deer pants for the water brooks, so pants my soul for You, O God. My soul thirsts for God, for the living God." – Psalm 42:1-2*

➤ *"For a day in Your courts is better than a thousand. I would rather be a doorkeeper in the house of my God than dwell in the tents of wickedness. For the Lord God is a sun and shield; the Lord will give grace and glory; no good thing will He withhold from those who walk uprightly." – Psalm 84:10-11*

We Show Up to Work

"And let us consider one another in order to stir up love and good works, not forsaking the assembling of ourselves together, as is the manner of some, but exhorting one another, and so much the more as you see the Day approaching." – Hebrews 10:24-25

The believer comes to church with the mission of stirring up love, provoking good works, and exhorting others. Not only do you come to church with a praise and a testimony, but you also bring forth a special ministry powered by a unique spiritual gift. When you exercise that gift, others are richly blessed.

Perhaps you are gifted with powerful prayer; when you pray for others, they are healed and delivered. Maybe you are blessed with a room-brightening smile; when you greet others, they are cheered and comforted. There are no "nobodies" in the church body—your presence makes a difference. Some say, "I really don't do much. They won't miss me if I stay home." Listen – you being here has a huge impact. In fact, 90 percent of success is just showing up!

In the 1500s in Europe, there was a church with no illumination. No lights. No windows. No Candelabra. Wanting to emphasize the importance of church attendance, the Mayor made a rule that everyone must bring their own lantern. At the end of each pew stood a space for people to hang their personal lanterns. Each person would come in with a lantern and place it in the receptacle. You can only imagine the effect: the greater the attendance, the brighter the sanctuary. If no one came, the church stood in total darkness. If only a few people came, the church was dimly lit. It was called "the house of many lamps."

When you are not at church, the light dims a little bit. Your showing up is important because you bring a light, a love, and a lift. The church needs you. When you are absent, you are missed.

The writer says that we must provoke each other in a good way. We must stir each other up in love. These are dangerous times and many are departing from the faith as is warned in verse 26, "For if we sin willfully after we have received the knowledge of the truth, there no longer remains a sacrifice for sins, but a certain fearful expectation of judgment, and fiery indignation which will devour the adversaries."

The writer is not speaking of a sin of weakness or a momentary surrender to fleshly temptation; the sin mentioned here is quite specific– the sin of apostasy. Some were guilty of this sin; they were leaving the church in total unbelief. They were rejecting the Gospel after once receiving it and were denying the Lord Jesus Christ. It was a total repudiation of Christianity. The writer says, "If you willingly sin like that and trample under your feet the blood of the covenant, then there is no salvation left for you."

If you leave the Christian church and go back into the world, you will find no salvation because God is not sending another Savior. If you reject the gospel of Christ, you will have no success in finding salvation in other places because God is not going to draw up another plan of salvation. Jesus Christ is the only Savior. If you walk away from Him and His church, there is no more sacrifice for sins. The only thing you can now look forward to is a certain and fearful judgment. This is a serious matter – we must continue in the faith. Only within the church can we find the strength, stability, and power to persevere in faith.

The early church fathers called God "Our Father" and the church "Our Mother." They believed that people could not have God for a Father without the church as a mother. Calvin said it this way: "There is no way

14

to enter into life unless this mother conceives us in her womb, nourishes us at her breast, and keeps us under her care and guidance."

The church was also likened to Noah's ark, a vehicle that saved from destruction. Albeit, church is not always fun—but neither was the ark. I'm sure some of Noah's family complained, "Daddy Noah, we don't like it in on this boat! I feel sea sick. I have no Dramamine. This is a floating zoo. The elephants won't shut up. The monkeys aren't that funny. The two mosquitoes keep biting me – why did their species have to be preserved? The lions are too loud. The snakes are scary. The skunks stink. In fact, the whole boat stinks." Noah would respond, "You have a choice: the stink or the storm." Personally, I would rather be on the safe, dry boat—even if it is filled with animals—than out in the storm where everyone is perishing.

The text instructs us to come together with exhortations, *especially* as we see the day approaching. As we get closer to the end time, the pressure will increase, trials and temptations will crescendo, and hostility will heat up. Many hearts will be deceived with sinfulness, but the church will provide the necessary strength to keep going in the truth!

Thus, "forsake not the gathering together." What a deadly danger that is! God is faithful to show up. He shows up with a truck filled with blessings: resources for our needs, answers to our prayers, strength for our lives, and provisions for our requests. The problem is, people are not showing up at the loading dock to collect the blessings. Let's be a showing up church!

A BIBLE BELIEVING CHURCH

2 Timothy 3:16-17

All Scripture is given by inspiration of God, and *is* profitable for doctrine, for reproof, for correction, for instruction in righteousness, that the man of God may be complete, thoroughly equipped for every good work.

I came across a fascinating article entitled "Favorite Facts That are False." This was really shocking to me. These were things I learned growing up and believed.

"Napoleon was short."
That's not true! He was 5'6". And that was slightly above average for the French men of his day.

"Don't eat and swim"
Have you heard that? That's not a problem, having a full stomach doesn't increase the risk of cramps. It might make it hard to breath. But you can go to the Golden Corral and then jump in the swimming pool, you're fine.

"Salty water boils quicker."
Have you heard that? That's not true. In fact, putting some salt in the water can make the boiling take longer.

"Dogs sweat by salivating."
No. They regulate their temperature by panting. But they actually sweat through their foot pads.

"Einstein failed math."
That's not true. He did fail an entrance exam into a specific school. But actually he was very good at math.

"Police require a 24-hour waiting period before accepting a missing person's report." That's not true. If somebody is missing from your family call the police immediately. They will go to work.

"Bananas grow on trees." No. Bananas grow on massive herbs that resemble trees.

"Bats are blind."
They are not. They can see. In fact they have a great built in radar system that makes them awesome.

"It takes seven years to digest gum."
That's not true. The chewy base of the gum is indigestible and it passes right through the body. The rest of it is absorbed into the body like other food.

"Bulls hate red."
Actually, bulls are color blind. They don't know what red is, but they are provoked by the motion of the cloth of the bull fighter.

Obviously, for some of these trivial matters we can believe wrong things and it's not a big deal. For some of these subjects, we may have the wrong information, but we will be alright. We want correct information about everything but some misinformation does not carry deadly consequences.

When it comes to spiritual things, we need to know the truth. We can't afford to believe a lie when it comes to spiritual things. False doctrine can damn the soul. The perverted philosophies of our world can poison the mind. We need the word of God to empower us to discern between truth and error. Oh, how we need discernment today! "The entrance of thy word giveth light" (Psalms 119:130). "Your word is a lamp unto my feet and a light unto my path" (Psalms 119:105).

There was a large denomination that hosted a conference to discuss, "Is the Bible really the Word of God?" We have never had a meeting like that at my church. We believe the Bible to be the inspired, infallible, inerrant, eternal, precious Word of God. And I'm not ashamed to believe it. I believe every word of the Book. In fact, I believe what is on the cover of the book - *Holy Bible*.

"All scripture is given by inspiration of God, and is profitable for doctrine, for reproof, for correction, for instruction in righteousness" (II Timothy 3:16).

That is a great word, **inspiration.** The formal definition goes like this, "The Holy Spirit overshadowed and superintendent the writers of Scripture, while persevering their individual personalities and their writing styles. They wrote under the influence of the Holy Spirit to the extent that they recorded accurately divine revelation and wrote what God wanted them to write."

The word **inspiration** literally means **God breathed**. God breathed out the very words of the Bible. Jesus said, "Man should not live by bread alone but by every word that proceeds from the mouth of God" (Matthew 4:4). We do need bread. I love bread! But man should not live on bread alone, because we are more than physical. We are more than flesh and blood. The Word of God gives us spiritual nourishment that truly satisfies

"Holy men spoke as they were moved by the Holy Spirit because prophecy did not originate in the will of man" (II Peter 1:21). The Bible did not come from the mind of man, it isn't a product of man's reasoning. God is not against reason, but His revelation is above reason. The Bible isn't a product of man's cleverness and creativity. "Holy men spoke as they were moved on by the Holy Spirit. The word **moved on** means they were **carried along**.

In Acts 27 there is a story about a ship with 276 passengers on the Aegean Sea. It got caught in such a bad storm, a hurricane. The ship was at the mercy of the wind. The wind determined the direction, the speed and the course of the ship. It was not in the hands of man to control and to navigate the ship—it was in power of the wind. The ship was borne along by the wind. The Holy Spirit is the wind of God. The writers of

Scripture, when they picked up the pen to write the Bible, they were so under the movement of the Spirit that the Holy Spirit determined what they would write.

What does that mean to be a Bible believing church? What does that look like?

Eternal Life through God's Word

"And that from a child thou hast known the holy scriptures, which are able to make thee wise unto salvation through faith which is in Christ Jesus."

— 2 Timothy 3:15

Jesus said, "You search the Scriptures, for in them you think you have eternal life; and these are they which testify of Me. But you are not willing to come to Me, that you may have life" (John 5:39-40).

Jesus was talking to the Pharisees. They loved Bible study. They enjoyed theological debate and discussions. They prided themselves that they were the custodians of orthodoxy. But they were under the illusion that they possessed spiritual life simply because they were Bible students and scholars. They did not understand that the entire Bible is a testimony of Jesus Christ.

It's not enough to own a Bible and enroll in a study group. We go to the Bible so we can learn the plan of salvation. Rather, that we can know the Man of salvation.

Do you know the name Elizabeth Browning? She married a man named Robert. The parents so disapproved of the union, it broke her heart. In fact, the parents were so angry at the marriage that they disowned her. Every week she sat down and wrote a letter to her parents, pleading for reconciliation. She tried to explain her love for Robert, and she asked them to please accept their union.

The letters are poetic, majestic and beautiful. The letters are now classics, beautiful letters in classical English literature. If you study English literature, you have to read the Robert Browning Letters. After ten years of marriage, a box arrived at Elizabeth's house and it deeply hurt her. She opened the box to find all her letters inside, they had been unopened. Never opened! The letters never effected the reconciliation. The letters never brought about the healing of the relationship, because the letters were never read. They were ignored and rejected.

God has given us a letter of reconciliation. "God was in Christ reconciling the world to himself" (II Corinthians 5). God has achieved the means for a complete reconciliation through the sacrificial death of Jesus Christ. The Bible is the letter that tells the story of love. But some never open up this love letter to learn about this redemptive story. They never experience the reconciliation that is proposed. The Bible's chief purpose is to bring us in faith to the Lord Jesus Christ that we might know a relationship with the true and living God.

Holy Worship through the Plain Teaching of Scripture

"But a time is coming and has now come when the true worshipers will worship the Father in spirit and in truth, for the Father is seeking such as these to worship Him. God is Spirit, and His worshipers must worship Him in spirit and in truth." – John 4:23-24

There is a right way to worship! The content to worship must be correct and the expression of worship must be correct. We can't free style it when it comes to worship.

In Leviticus 10 we read about the two sons of Aaron. These "PK's" or **preachers kids** were getting into trouble way back then. These two boys, Nadab and Abihu, they had the manual on worship. They knew the right procedures for acceptable worship. The incense had to be mixed right. There were certain amounts of spices that were specified. A certain number of quarts of oil were poured into the mix. There was a right way to offer incense on the altar. There was a right place and proper utensils. But the two sons of Aaron came up with their own recipe. "We don't need God's cookbook," they thought. "We will do our own thing." How did that work for them? Fire came out from the altar and struck them dead.

I think it is plain that God has opinions about how we worship. As pastor of a church, I'm a quite zealous and jealous about how we worship. It's not to be grouchy and fussy. I don't want God to strike me dead with fire! Everything we do in church must have a biblical basis. Even church traditions must be evaluated to determine if they really reflect Bible ideas and principles. We must constantly measure our worship against the standards of the Bible.

Spiritual Revival through the Faithful Preaching of God's Word

---

"Preach the word; be prepared in season and out of season; reprove, rebuke, and encourage with every form of patient instruction." – 2 Timothy 4:2

A lot of churches are out of the preaching business—they're done. They think revival comes another way. They think evangelism comes another way. I visited a church that didn't have a pulpit. They had three high chairs on the stage and the staff sat on those chairs and engaged in discussion. I went to another church that did not deliver a sermon, they showed a video and presented a skit. There are ways to communicate truth through other mediums. I'm not trying to belittle drama, or videos, or a discussion.

Nothing takes the place of the preaching of God's Word. This is not just

21

something we are doing because a tradition was handed down through the years. It's not something we do because clergy need a job. It's not something we do because we thought about it and concluded that this is a good way to reach people. We preach because that is what God has ordained. This is what God promises to bless! He chose the foolishness of preaching to save those who are believing (I Corinthians 1:21).

Sometimes a preacher can get discouraged when he surveys the spiritual death that surrounds him. This is why ministers need to take courage from Ezekiel 37. Ezekiel was taken down to the valley of dry bones and observed that "there were very many bones and they were very dry" (Ezekiel 37:2). God told Ezekiel, that this is going to be his place of ministry.

I don't know what had happened in that valley, but there was a destruction. There was a wipeout. Those who attacked didn't even have the respect to bury these human beings. The victims were so picked over, the vultures were not even flying overhead. This was a scene of defeat and destruction. No potential for life.

I look at our culture and I'm shocked at how far people have gone away from God. Such an extreme secularism has gripped Americans and we wonder if there is hope. We look at other parts of the world and we see false religion and darkness, and we wonder if there is hope for these countries. Even mainline denominations are now in a state of compromise. Of churches today, 80% have either plateaued or are now in decline of attendance.

There's a valley of dry bones all around us. What's the answer? What is the remedy? What do we do? God said to Ezekiel, "Start preaching to the bones." Talk about crazy! Preach to the bones? They don't even have ears. God told Ezekiel to preach and prophecy to the bones.

I started preaching when I was ten years old. I got a few invitations to speak at churches when I was young. It was kind of cute-little Timmy preaching! It was kind of a novelty for some churches to hear me, but God was using me in a serous way. I wanted more opportunities than what was opening for me. I wanted to preach so badly. The fire was burning in my heart.

I'll never forget one day, I went into my bedroom and lined up my stuffed animals—a lion, a bear, and a tiger. I lined them all up on the edge of the bed just like church members sitting in pews. I took a magic marker for my microphone and I started preaching to these stuffed animals. They were just staring at me. I tell you, I was preaching with energy.

At some point in the sermon, I felt so much of the power of God, I literally took my hand and laid my hand on each stuffed animal thinking they would come to life. I don't know what I would have done if they had come to life, but preaching always fascinated me because I sensed that God would bless it.

Can you imagine Ezekiel in the worst conditions? These weren't stuffed animals, they were dead and dried bones. But Ezekiel obeyed and began to preach. He had no choir to back him up. He had no praise and worship band to set the mood. He had no ushers and greeters to make people feel welcome. He had no stained glass windows to encourage spiritual thoughts. He had no pot luck dinner to excite attendance. He had nothing but the pure preaching of the Word of God.

He preached and suddenly there was a rattling, there was a shaking. The knee bone connecting to the thigh bone. The thigh bone connected to the hip bone. The bones came together in a proper order. The Word of God brought connection, order and the right relationships.

Not only bones were coming back to where they belonged, but then tissue and muscles, sinew and flesh got attached to the skeletons. Soon, human bodies appeared all over the valley. You know what this was? It was a reversal of the process of decomposition. It was going back in time. It was re-doing what tragedy had taken place in the valley. There had been massive destruction in that valley prior to the preaching of the Word. But now, under the voice of the prophet, everything was rolling back.

It's not enough to have bodies human assembled correctly, if they are still dead. Who cares if there is a pretty ear, but it can't hear? Who cares if there is an eye in the eye socket, if it can't see? Who cares if there is a well formed mouth, if the mouth can't speak? Who cares if the heart has four nice chambers, but can't pump blood? Who cares if the hand is

23

sculptured just right, but it can't move? The human bodies needed the miracle of life!

So then God said to Ezekiel, "You must now preach a second sermon—preach to the wind. Preach about the Holy Ghost." Ezekiel called for the breath of God to fill that valley and impart life into those corpses. And all of a sudden, there was a wind blowing and those dead bodies got up with life in them, and there was an exceeding great army.

Is there hope for America? Preach the word! Is there hope for main line denomination gone into compromising corruption? Preach the word! Is there hope for nations that are bound by false religion? Preach the word! Is there hope for a generation that seems to be filled with spiritual death? Preach the word!

Personal Growth through the Transforming Power of God's Word

"For the word of God is alive and active. Sharper than any double-edged sword, it penetrates even to dividing soul and spirit, joints and marrow; it judges the thoughts and attitudes of the heart".
Hebrew 4:12

The Word of God not only changes our culture and our churches, the Word of God can transform our personal lives! The Bible is a discerner of the thoughts and intents of the heart. When we read the Bible, it actually reads us. We don't know ourselves—that's the problem. We really don't know ourselves.

If a group of people are together and one person is singing off-key, who's the last person to know? In a group of people, somebody has irritating mannerisms and who's the last person to know? In a group of people, if a person is talking too much, who's is the last person to know? We miss the obvious. We miss the obvious about ourselves.

Sherlock Holmes and Dr. Watson were on a camping trip. Sherlock Holmes nudged Watson in the middle of the night. They looked up and saw the stars. Sherlock said to Watson, "What do you see?" He replied, "I see stars." Sherlock asked "What do you inter from that?" Sherlock answered, "Astronomically, there's billions of galaxies, billions of stars and planets. Meteorologically, it's going to be a bright and beautiful day when the sun rises. Chronologically, it's 2:30 am right now. Theologically, God is great. How about you my dear Watson, who do you conclude?" To that, Watson replied, "Somebody stole our tent."

We miss the obvious. We need this Bible to function as a mirror that we might see our true selves. That can be discouraging. But the Bible is also likened unto water - a cleansing agent. The same Bible that reveals our dirt will provide the cleansing power to wash away that dirt.

One of my favorite stories is *The Chronicles of Narnia* by C.S. Lewis. It's about a little boy named Eustace. He turned into a dragon. Here, Lewis is trying to show that sin is dehumanizing.

Aslan is a type of Christ. Aslan was to help the boy and give him a new birth - a new beginning. The boy had to peel off that dragon skin. He tried, and it was crusty and ugly. He peeled off one layer and it hurt so badly, but there was another layer underneath. It was like an onion, it kept peeling, but it was never gone. So then he thought, "I can't change myself."

Aslan said, "You can't change yourself, but now you know the depth of your dragon nature. I have to change you. Son, are going to let me change you?" Eustace said "Yes." He laid down and got still. Eustace was frightened by the claws of the lion. The first tear was so deep and he feared that he could not take this kind of surgery but the lion proved to be tender and skillful.

Soon Eustace sensed that it felt good to get rid of that crusty mess. Then finally, it was gone and he laid there naked. The lion lifted him up and he took him to a pool. He dipped the boy in the water, at first it was a little painful but then it was delicious. After a few minutes the boy was splashing and swimming and he felt clean and reborn. He was happy because he looked like a boy again.

When God saves you, he accepts you the way you are, dragon and all. But then He takes the surgical knife of the Word and begins to rip away the layers of sin. Only He can change us. Yes, sometimes there is pain. But mostly there is relief and joy that the ugliness of sin is being removed. How glorious to be reshaped into the beautiful image of Christ.

A SACRAMENTAL CHURCH

Acts 2:38-42

Then Peter said to them, "Repent and let every one of you be baptized in the name of Jesus Christ for the remission of sins; and you shall receive the gift of the Holy Spirit. For the promise is to you and to your children, and to all who are afar off, as many as the Lord our God will call." And with many other words he testified and exhorted them, saying, "Be saved from this perverse generation." Then those who gladly received his word were baptized; and that day about three thousand souls were added to them. And they continued steadfastly in the apostles' doctrine and fellowship, in the breaking of bread, and in prayers.

I have a friend who pastors a church in Birmingham, Alabama. A few years ago, when his children were small, the family was taking a drive, and they were listening to the radio. Suddenly, the song "Let's Get Physical" came on. You remember that song by Olivia Newton John: "Let's get physical, physical!" My friend gently turned it off, thinking it might not be the best song for little children. Unfortunately, he was too late.

"Daddy, what does that mean? Let's get physical?" his six year old girl asked. My friend gulped real big. Then, the eight year old son spoke up and said to his sister, "I will tell you what it means." Now my friend gulped real big! The son proceeded to explain the terminology to his sister: "Let's get physical— that is what happens when the Alabama Crimson Tide football team plays Auburn on a Saturday afternoon in Tuscaloosa." My friend, quite relieved, sighed deeply.

It's important that we define things properly – especially things that are physical. There are two physical activities in the church that are ordained by Christ that have special spiritual significance. We are talking about the two blessed sacraments: Water Baptism and Holy Communion. Some Christians really struggle with the idea that a physical act could be so spiritual. How can a material rite affect moral reality and communicate spiritual graces? Getting baptized is so physical—you are getting wet! You feel the physicality of it! And Holy Communion is so plain and simple—you taste the bread and wine. You place food in the mouth, you chew, and you swallow.

Can God really be imparted through something so physical? The answer is **yes.** True Christianity does not make a dichotomy between the physical and spiritual. The old heresy of Gnosticism labeled everything physical and sensual as evil. The sacraments remind us that God made the physical world; furthermore, the Word became flesh and dwelt among us (John 1:14). God wants to participate in every human aspect of our lives; play, work, making money, having fun, romantic relationships, laughing, friendships, enjoying nature, suffering, and crying. God is not distant to our physical lives, and He reminds us of that truth by placing within the experience of holy worship two physical actions. He then turns these physical actions into amazing and mysterious spiritual impartations.

The word sacrament is defined as "an outward and visible sign of an inward and spiritual grace." God is so great in His love and care for His people that He calls us into the fellowship of His divine Son and assures us of His good will! To do this, He established two simple activities that become channels of grace. He has bound Himself to these sacraments in such a way that we become partakers of His powerful works of redemption. Let's be precise and very clear as we define the meaning of these sacraments. How can we understand, "Let's get physical?"

The Sacraments are Sacred Symbols

The Old Covenant that God established with Israel was marked with two special signs: Circumcision and the Passover meal. Circumcision was the sign of initiation through which the entire family embraced the covenant with God. Faith was a family affair. When the son turned eight days old, he entered into this holy ceremony of circumcision, becoming a member of the covenant family of faith.

As a side note, it is interesting to observe an article that came out in a medical journal concerning the safest day to circumcise a baby. It explained that on the eighth day of a boy's life, he has more vitamin K, a blood clotting agent, in his body than on any other day of his life - making the eighth day the safest day. God knew that. That's why He commanded circumcision to be performed on that day. The skin was cut, the blood was shed, and the boy bore the mark of being a true Jew in special relationship with God.

In the New Covenant, circumcision is replaced with baptism. Baptism is the sign that brings us into the family of God and seals us with a heavenly mark of public identification with Jesus Christ.

> ➤ "For as many of you as were baptized into Christ have put on Christ. There is neither Jew nor Greek, there is neither slave nor free, there is neither male nor female; for you are all one in Christ Jesus." – Galatians 3:27-28

> ➤ "In Him you were also circumcised with the circumcision made without hands, by putting off the body of the sins of the flesh, by the circumcision of Christ, buried with Him in baptism, in which you also were raised with Him through faith in the working of God, who raised Him from the dead." – Colossians 2:11-12

In the New Covenant, just as baptism replaces circumcision, so the Passover meal is replaced with the Lord's Supper. The Jewish people gathered annually to share a special meal commemorating their deliverance from Egypt's bondage. Remember how God made the promise, "When I see the blood, my judgment will pass over you." Pass

- over! Sometimes we don't like the words "pass over." When we are at work and want a promotion or a bonus – we surely don't' want to be passed over. But when it comes to the judgment of sin, we want to be passed over.

What a blessed promise: "I will pass over you." Jewish families took the blood of the lamb and painted it on the door post. When the death angel visited on that fateful night in Egypt, it did not enter the blood-sprinkled houses to slay the first born children. The lamb had already been slain as a substitute, and the visible blood provided evidence of that sacrificial death. When the death angel saw the blood, he passed over and went on down the road.

The Passover meal was a wonderful fellowship with God's redeemed people to remember salvation, deliverance, mercy, and special favor. Jesus was sitting with His disciples in the upper room enjoying Passover when suddenly He shocked them with these words: "Take eat—this is my body. Drink the cup, for this is my blood of the new covenant which is shed for many for the remission of sins" (Matthew 26:26-28). Jesus replaced the Passover with the Lord's Supper.

Baptism and the Lord's Supper serve as the two signs of the New Covenant. Since these are sacred and instituted by Christ, we do not have the flexibility to tamper with them. We do not have the liberty to change them, delete them, amend them, or improve them.

Some churches have little esteem for these sacraments and push them to the peripheral. They may have a water baptism once a year on a Sunday night after the congregation has been dismissed. They might have Holy Communion once a year on a rainy night when only a few people can attend. Others think we need to be contemporary and modernize the sacraments.

One church offers Twinkies and Coca-Cola instead of bread and wine. One pastor said, "I have a better idea than water baptism to illustrate salvation. I want to build a little closet on the church platform. The convert can enter the closet with old clothes, change his clothes inside the closet, and then emerge in new clothes. That makes more sense that baptism." No my friends! We better not mess with God's sacred signs.

Some churches see the sacraments as ancient practices that need to be relegated to the museum of faith, assuming the sacraments have lost their value and relevance in our modern world. I know one church that places the administration of baptism in the category of Traditional Christian Worship at the early Sunday service for those who like "the old time religion."

For some, the sacraments are seen as an inconvenience. I remember a lady in my church who claimed salvation but would never get baptized because she did not want her long, pretty blond hair to get wet in public.

The sacraments are not old relics of the past that need to be scrapped. They are not nuisances that we must endure. They are not church activities subject to man's manipulation and control. They are gracious and powerful gifts from God that must be protected and presented. We must do God's work, God's way.

When it comes to baptism, the formula is important – we use a Trinitarian formula in baptism. Jesus said, "Go therefore and make disciples of all nations, baptizing them in the name of the Father and of the Son and of the Holy Spirit" (Matthew 28:19).

The Book of Acts states that people were baptized into the name of Jesus Christ. But that does not mean they ignored the Trinitarian words. It was Luke's way of stating that it was a Christian baptism. The fact that people were baptized in the name of Jesus meant that they were baptized with the authority of Christ. They must have obeyed Him and used the Trinitarian formula prescribed.

The mode is also important—we baptize by immersion because that was the New Testament way! The Ethiopian dignitary was listening to Deacon Philip preach Christ from the book of Isaiah as they bumped on down the desert highway sitting in the back of a chariot. The dignitary received the Word in faith and said to Phillip, "Hey, look! There is much water right there. Can I stop this chariot and get baptized?" He did not ask, "Philip, do you have a bottle of water in your pocket that you can pour over my head?" No! He knew the way baptism was done. He knew he needed a lot of water. As our example, Jesus Himself "came up out of the water" (Mark 1:10).

The word "baptize" itself means to be immersed. Let's not change the plan: baptism pictures the death, burial, and resurrection of Christ and our participation in those great historical events. If we baptize with sprinkling or pouring, then we change the picture. My baptism was the funeral of the old man. I wore a robe. My hands were folded. I was lowered back into the water, a liquid tomb. I disappeared under the water. That was my death, and the only mourner at that funeral was the devil. He hated to see the old Timothy die. When Luther would be tempted of the devil, he had a powerful way of overcoming. He would tell the devil, "Be gone Satan, I am a baptized man. The old Luther died a long time ago." Yes, my baptism was my funeral, and the devil was crying. I was happy because the nasty Timmy was buried, and a new Timmy, resurrected in the likeness of Christ, emerged from the water.

Do you see how the baptismal mode of immersion demonstrates the beauty of the work of Christ and how we enter into that work? Suppose you have never seen my children and ask me, "Can I see a picture of your children?" I pull out a picture of a racecar instead. Shocked, you would argue that the picture is not even of humans, much less my children. "Oh, any picture will do," I respond. No! Any picture will *not* do.

We are not to tamper with Baptism or Holy Communion. I know one minister on television who sells communion kits, he calls communion "the meal that heals." He instructs individuals to serve Communion to themselves in the privacy of their homes and to claim divine healing. No! We are not to remove Holy Communion from the fellowship of the church and from the protection of ordained ministers. We are not to turn it into some sales item that guarantees physical health. In I Corinthians 11 we learn that church members suffered severe judgment because they did not participate in Holy Communion in a proper way. The sacraments are sacred signs that must be protected from foolishness and carnal manipulation. They are two visible marks of our covenant relationship with God.

Baptism gets us into the family, and the Supper keeps us in the family. Baptism is initiation, and the Supper is nourishment.

The Sacraments are Simple Symbols

I am using the word "simple" to give us balance in our view of the sacraments. Some churches like to elevate the sacraments into something they are not ordained to be. Some churches diminish the sacraments, but other churches deify the sacraments. There are many churches that turn the sacraments into something magical, asserting that the sacraments contain the power to save and sanctify in and of themselves.

The belief is that the symbols automatically impart spiritual grace to the recipient regardless of the attitude and faith of the recipient. On the contrary, the person participating in the sacraments must have personal faith in Christ, or the ritual becomes an empty ritual.

There are some who get into the baptismal pool a dry sinner and come out a wet sinner. Why? Because the one being baptized did not have faith in the blood of Jesus Christ. We are not saved by the water, but we are saved by the Man who tells us to get into the water. We must have a cleansing agent that goes deeper than skin.

The song says, "There is a fountain filled with blood, drawn from Immanuel's veins. And sinners plunged beneath the flood lose all their guilty stain." It is not the water that washes away sin, but the blood of Jesus Christ that washes away sin.

The sacraments do not impart the blessings of God in a mechanical and magical way apart from the work of the Holy Spirit. The Spirit must minister to those who are exercising faith in the Lord Jesus Christ. If we come to the Lord's Table without spiritual connection with the living Christ, then our eating and drinking is in vain. The sacraments have no saving profit if one is refusing the Savior that is offered in the sacraments.

The sacraments are **simple** in that they are distinct from the reality they represent. Some churches call the bread the Host, meaning this is actually "Christ," and they bow down before the bread and worship it. Some churches will not even offer wine to the congregation because they believe it to be the actual blood of Jesus, and the risk of spilling that wine and splashing the blood of Jesus Christ on the floor is too hideous and blasphemous. Some teach that if even a mouse eats a crumb from the Lord's Table, then that little creature will have eternal life. These various beliefs confuse the sign from the thing signified.

When the bread and wine are consecrated in prayer, they become sacred symbols, meant to communicate Christ to us as we worship in spirit and in truth. Nonetheless, the bread remains bread. The wine remains wine. The properties of the elements do not change.

When the water in the pool is consecrated through prayer, that water still remains as H_2O. It does not magically change into another substance. If we do not remember that sacraments are symbols, then we might be guilt of idolatry in worship.

The Sacraments are Spiritual Symbols

Confusing the symbol with the thing signified is a dangerous error, but there is also a danger of separating the symbol from the thing signified to the degree that it becomes an empty, naked symbol. The sacraments are not empty, externally religious rites that are void of vitality and power.

The sacraments are united to the reality, welded by the power of the Spirit. God performs a saving work in the pool of baptism and a sanctifying work at the Lord's Table. These are the two arenas of God's redemptive activity as He confirms His Word to us and seals His promises to us.

The bath and the table are homely, family-oriented images. Taking a bath! Pulling your chair up at the table for a meal! We are the family of God and God blesses His children through the symbols that make us think of home. But these symbols are much more than play-acting and thinking back to fonder days back home, they are activities that connect the believer with the resources and riches of God's grace. This is why the Bible speaks of the sacraments in terms of the realities they represent. This is called the language of sacramentalism.

Baptism is a powerful act of worship when the Holy Spirit is ministering the benefits of the Cross to the person exercising faith.

> ➤ *"Do you not know that as many of us as were baptized into Christ Jesus were baptized into His death?" – Romans 6:3*

> ➤ *"For as many of you as were baptized into Christ have put on Christ." – Galatians 3:27*

Baptism is not a naked symbol. Even our text demonstrates the power of baptism as an instrument to cleanse the soul, "Repent and be baptized and you shall receive the forgiveness of sins and the gift of the Holy Spirit."

Holy Communion is instrumental in the believer taking hold of the living Christ and the Holy Spirit applying the blessings of the Cross to the believing heart.

> ➤ *Jesus distributed the bread and announced, "This is my body." He shared the cup and declared "This is my blood."*

> ➤ *He tells us in John 6:54, "Whoever eats My flesh and drinks My blood has eternal life, and I will raise him up at the last day."*

Holy Communion is more than a memorial meal, a birthday cake, or a visual reminder. The real activity of Holy Communion is not a mental exercise where we strain our brains, trying to recall historical events or understand Christ's death on a simply intellectual level.

Communion promises the presence of Christ in a measure and manner that we cannot know Him outside the Supper. Communion is not the labor of the mind; it is the relaxed and obedient heart that humbly enters into a fresh experience of Calvary through the power of the Holy Spirit.

In I Corinthians 10:20, Paul said that when pagans go to the temple and offer sacrifices to idols, they are actually having an intimate fellowship with demons. There is an energy in that room. There is direct contact with the unseen, demonized world. Then, Paul makes a comparison between that perverted worship and holy worship- "You cannot drink of the cup of the Lord and the cup of demons. You cannot partake of the Lord's table and the table of demons" (I Corinthians 10:21).

Holy Communion escorts us into the spiritual world of grace, and we receive divine energy as we partake of the risen Christ who died for us, who lives for us, and who will come again for us. We eagerly, expectantly, regularly, and reverently participate in the sacraments because they are visible signs of invisible grace. Furthermore, they are sanctified channels through which we receive saving and sustaining grace as they confirm the promises of the gospel that are presented in the preached Word.

A CREEDAL CHURCH

> ## II Timothy 1:13
>
> "Hold fast the pattern of sound words which you have heard from me, in faith and love which are in Christ Jesus."

Why did the horses get a divorce? They did not have a stable relationship!

There is a great stability that comes into our lives as we get anchored into faith. This is the value of creeds.

"I Believe" We hear those words every day. Whatever the context, we want to tell others what we are thinking and what convictions capture our hearts and what affections direct our behavior. A few years ago in Baltimore they took the word "believe" and turned it into a motto to lift the spirits of those in the city. So all through the city you see that word plastered on buildings, etched on benches and expressed on banners.

In the Christmas movie, Polar Express, you find there is a key word for the little boy to enter into the joys and magic of Christmas - "believe." I like the word "believe." But the real big question is not "Do you believe?" We all believe in something. The big question is, "In what do you believe?" Your faith is only as good as its object.

Historically, the church has used creeds because the church is the pillar and ground of truth. The church is prominently a confessional community. We confess precious and powerful Bible truths. The church where I pastor, we use the Nicene Creed when we baptize converts. When we partake of Holy Communion we recite the Apostle's Creed. We use the Westminster Confession for the pedagogical training of our children.

"I believe." Creeds are confessions to summarize and express the basic beliefs of Christianity. They have been constructed throughout the 2,000 years of church history by people from different places and contexts, but who are all bound together by the shared horizon of God's revelation in Christ as recorded in sacred Scripture. These creeds transcend local conditions and connect us with people and ages that are far removed from us.

Creeds are not canonical. We do not place them on the same shelf as the Holy Bible and declare them to be infallible. Like traditions that are passed down to us, they are subject to correction. But they prove to be a valuable instrument to support Scripture, preserve sound doctrine, teach our young, humble us in appreciation for a long history of Christian testimony, and to join us with hearts of Christians around the world.

There are some churches that have no use for the creeds. They say, "No creed, but the Bible." Of course, that statement is a kind of creed. We all have our creeds – whether they are formal or informal; new or old. We all filter the content of the Bible into some kind of intelligible belief system and then attempt to express that summary to others. So really, every church is creedal. I feel much safer taking the creeds that date back to the dawn of Christianity, creeds that are tried and proven.

Actually, the Bible actually encourages us to formulate some creeds. II Tim 1:13, "Hold fast the form of sound words, which thou has heard of me, in faith and love which is in Christ Jesus." The ESV renders it this way, "Follow the pattern of the sound words that you have heard from me, in the faith and love that are in Christ." The word **form** describes a model or standard that is intended to function as a trustworthy and reliable guide.

The Bible makes several references to popular sayings or creeds that were used in worship in the primitive church. I Timothy 1:15, "This statement is trustworthy a deserving of all acceptance, that Christ Jesus came into the world to save sinners." This was an early creed! When churches gathered on the Lord's Day the congregation would recite in unison, "Christ Jesus came into the world to save sinners." Paul heard it and endorsed it. He said, "I like that creed. I like the words to that. That is worthy of you officially accepting that into your liturgy of worship."

There are other passages of Scripture that have a creedal tone. An example is I Timothy 3:16, "God was manifested in the flesh, justified in the Spirit, seen by angels, preached among the gentiles, believed on in the world, received up into glory." I wish I had time to dissect this passage because it is filled with literary genius and poetic eloquence. But it was a popular saying that helped the church focus on the mystery and main substance of the Christian message. It was a creed. Paul takes it into the Bible and blesses it.

Let me share with you four reasons why we should incorporate the ancient creeds into modern worship.

We Need Creeds to Clarify Doctrine

A Christian man was asked at his work office, "What do you believe?" He said, "I believe what my church believes." "Oh, and what does your church believe?" The Christian answered, "They believe what I believe." "Nice. And what do you and your church believe?" The Christian said, "We believe the same thing."

Do we know what we believe? The Bible is so big! It contains 66 books that cover a time span of 1500 years. The story stretches over that vast arena of time and the doctrinal statements are scattered all over the place. It is difficult to get precise about our doctrinal positions. That is why we have creeds. Creeds don't supplement the Bible, but they do serve the Bible in helping us to draw from Scripture the main ideas that are crucial to Christianity.

Some not only despise creeds, but they despise doctrines. I heard a person say, "No Creed, but Christ." That may sound so spiritual and nice. But when you say "Christ" you are making a doctrinal statement. What does Christ mean? What is His mission? Who is He? There are many false Christ's – how can we recognize the true Christ?

Obviously, we need doctrine. And yes we need creeds to empower us to capsulate essential truth and to show a coherent and unified understanding of the whole scope of Scripture. The creeds being simple and short help us to memorize the key doctrinal positions of the Bible. What a blessing!

We Need Creeds Construct Christianity

Matthew 16 is so important because it shows us the relationship between correct belief and the development of Christianity. When Jesus first mentioned that He would start a church, He did it in response to a confession that came from the mouth of Simon Peter. Jesus had taken His disciples far north to a place called Caesarea. Philip had erected a monumental temple that was resplendent in white marble, massive in size, and dedicated to the worship of the many gods of Rome. The city was built to celebrate the Greek god Pan. Pan speaks of expansiveness.

Panorama – you know that word. It refers to a view that gives you a wide vision. Pan brought together the seductive superstition of the Orient, the heady philosophies of Greece, the military might of the Romans, the idols of all cultures. It was a celebration of religious diversity.

Jesus brought His Twelve to the base of this pagan temple and He asked them, "Who do you say that I am?" It was Peter who, with the temple of Pan casting a shadow over his shoulders, spoke up to articulate the great truth concerning Christ. So this was the original Peter Pan. The Spirit of God fell upon Peter and he reverently responded "Thou art the Christ the Son of the Living God." Jesus answered, "Flesh and blood has not revealed this to you, but My Father has revealed this to you. Peter you are a stone, and upon this rock I will build my church and the gates of hell shall not prevail against it" (Matthew16:17-18).

Some people are embarrassed by creeds because they are narrow. "It's not nice to be narrow." When I fly by airplane I am so happy that the pilot is narrow enough to land the plane on the runway.

There is a very specific belief system that forms the foundation for Christianity. Historically, those who came to the pool for water baptism, they were asked a series of questions: "Do you believe in God the Father Almighty? Do you believe in Jesus Christ, Son of God, who was born of the virgin Mary, who was crucified under Pontius Pilate, and died, and rose on the third day and ascended into heaven? Do you believe in the Holy Spirit, the Holy Christian Church, the resurrection of the dead?" You may say, "Hey, that sounds just like the Apostle's Creed." Bingo! That is how we got the Apostle's Creed. It started out as a series of questions for candidates for baptism.

Christianity started with a confession. You start your Christian journey with a confession. You continue your daily life of discipleship with confession. Jesus says in Matthew 10:32, "Whoever confesses Me before men, him will I confess before My Father who is in heaven."

As Christians, we must hold on to our confession till the end of time. Hebrews 10:23, "Let us hold to the confession of our hope without wavering, for He who promised is faithful." Hebrews 4:14, "Seeing then that we have a high priest who has passed into the heavens, Jesus the Son of God, let us hold fast our confession."

Get a bull dog grip on the confession of faith and don't let go. But don't hold it so tightly that you don't pass it on. We pass the torch on. Jude exhorted, "Contend for the faith that was once and for all delivered to the saints" (Jude 3).

When ministers were ordained and set forth for public service, the ceremony was filled with creeds. Because one of the chief responsibilities of the minister is to guard the faith and to pass it on to a new generation.

In many church traditions today the creeds are read after the sermon is delivered. Why? To hold that minister accountable. The church is checking the content of his sermon against sound doctrine. "Did the sermon today stay within biblical bounds?"

God uses the pure confession of faith to construct His church, develop His people, propagate His message, establish His presence in a community, and prepare humanity for eternity.

41

We Need Creeds to Confirm Unity

Our unity is grounded in doctrinal truth. (Ephesians 4:3-5)

We cannot have peace at any price. True Christianity unity is built on truth. But we must recognize that there are two categories of doctrinal truth. First, there are doctrinal truths that are primary and necessary. Secondly, there are doctrinal truths that are secondary and non-essential. Sometimes we fight and fuss over doctrines that should not rupture our fellowship. I have many Christian friends who disagree with me concerning the timing of the rapture. But that is a secondary doctrinal position. It is important, but not essential for being a Christian.

The creeds focus on those primary and essential doctrines that identity us as truly Christian. This banner of truth should bring all of God's people into a loving fellowship of common cause. My particular congregation is of the pre-millennial persuasion. The church down the street from us is of the post-millennial conviction. But we can respect those differences and fellowship as brothers and sisters in Christ. Why? Because both congregations can rise up on Sunday morning and recite the Apostle's Creed.

Now this is a doubled edged sword, because while creeds celebrate and confirm unity, it also corrects error and gives us power of discernment. In fact, most the creeds were born out of a battle with heretics.

The Nicene Creed was written because of a heretical attack. A man by the name of Arius was teaching that Jesus Christ was a created being and so He was not full deity; He was less than God in essence. Hundreds of Bishops gathered in Nicea in 325 to discuss the matter. They prayed and searched the Scriptures. Arius had become quite popular and many followed his teachings. This was a real threat to Christianity.

Finally, the council concluded the matter with a denunciation of the teachings of Arius and a new creed was born. The creed helps us to think straight with our Christology. The words were carefully and prayerfully chosen to reflect what the Bible teaches about our wonderful Lord and Savior.

Nicene Creed

"I believe in one Lord Jesus Christ, the only begotten Son of God, begotten of His Father before all worlds, God of God, Light of Light, very God of very God, begotten, not made, being of one substance with the Father, by whom all things were made, who for us men and for our salvation came down from heaven, and was incarnate by the Holy Spirit of the Virgin Mary, and was made man, and crucified under Pontius Pilate; He suffered, died and was buried and the third day He rose again according to the Scriptures, and ascended into heaven and sitteth on the right hand of the Father and He shall come again with glory to judge both the quick and the dead; Whose kingdom shall have no end."

Creeds affirm and celebrate the true unity of the church while protecting us from heretical intrusions and false Christ's.

We Need Creeds to Crown Worship

Some do not favor creeds because they seem too cerebral and propositional. I mean, they are dusty and dry old documents. What does this have to do with the passion of praise and worship?

It is fascinating to observe how Paul was always turning doctrine into doxology. The deep truths of the gospel were the driving force behind his emotions of worship. True praise rises out of a an accurate understanding of who God is and thanksgiving flows out of a heart that knows the story of redemption and can rehearse what God has done for us.

When you praise your wife, it is not a general expression of vague compliments. That doesn't work. No! You have to get real specific with detailed descriptives. You are sitting at the dining table with soft music playing and candle burning. You look across the table and you say, "Oh darling, your eyes are deep and blue like the mysteries of the ocean. Your hair is flowing and lying softly on your shoulders like the gentle leaves descending in autumn. Your skin is so clear and clean, I am almost hesitant to touch such soft silk lest I ruffle perfection." Now that is an expression that the wife will really appreciate. It flows out of a heart of love that has deeply discerned the beauty of the wife in specificity. It is much more meaningful than, "Hey woman – you look good." Our worship to God is not just some general recognition that there is a higher power up there somewhere. We know Him as God the Maker, God the Father, God the covenant keeper, God who sent His Son, and God who loves his people.

When the early church recited the creeds, there was nothing boring, routine or dry about it. In fact, here was an early creed that actually had some music to it. It was more of a hymn. But the early church loved this statement of faith because it made them think correctly about Jesus and it gave them practical instruction about following Jesus. When they shared this in worship it was with joy, smiles, shouting, inflexions, head shaking, jumping, bowing, and kneeling.

Imagine a first century congregation joyfully shouting these words, "Who being in the form of God, did not consider it robbery to be equal with God, but made Himself of no reputation, taking the form of a bondservant, and coming in the likeness of men. And being found in appearance as a man, He humbled Himself and became obedient to the point of death, even the death of the cross. Therefore, God also has highly exalted Him and given Him the name which is above every name, that at the name of Jesus every knee should bow, of those in heaven, and of those on earth, and of those under the earth, and that every tongue should confess that Jesus Christ is Lord, to the glory of God the Father" (Philippians 2:6-11).

The creeds will help us put substance to our worship so that we won't depend on high emotions and staged cheer-leaders to get us whipped up into the excitement of worship. Worship is a heart-felt response to the revelation of God and the creeds help us to discern the heart of that revelation and give us the power to participate in its expressions in an orderly, joyful and unified manner.

Oh – Let us restore the creeds to our worship experience!

A RESOURCEFUL CHURCH

2 Kings 4:1-7

Now there cried a certain woman of the wives of the sons of the prophets unto Elisha, saying, Thy servant my husband is dead; and thou knowest that thy servant did fear the LORD: and the creditor is come to take unto him my two sons to be bondmen. And Elisha said unto her, What shall I do for thee? tell me, what hast thou in the house? And she said, Thine handmaid hath not anything in the house, save a pot of oil. Then he said, Go, borrow thee vessels abroad of all thy neighbors, even empty vessels; borrow not a few. And when thou art come in, thou shalt shut the door upon thee and upon thy sons, and shalt pour out into all those vessels, and thou shalt set aside that which is full. So she went from him, and shut the door upon her and upon her sons, who brought the vessels to her; and she poured out. And it came to pass, when the vessels were full, that she said unto her son, Bring me yet a vessel. And he said unto her, There is not a vessel more. And the oil stayed. Then she came and told the man of God. And he said, Go, sell the oil, and pay thy debt, and live thou and thy children of the rest.

When we venture out to do the work of God, there will always be needs and challenges, but God is more than enough. He sends us resources so we can be sufficient for the mission He has for us. We are going to talk about God's sufficiency for the challenges that you face in your life. I love the story in 2 Kings 4. He took what the widow had, which was not a lot, and multiplied it. How do we release our resources?

I have some questions for you to ponder. How many of you would like to have love in your life? In 1 Corinthians 13, Paul says you can have knowledge and prophecy and faith and gifts. But if you don't have love, you're nothing. I want love in my life.

How many would like to have power in your life? We need power to really make a difference in the world. We need power to make a lasting impression for God. We need power to reach our goals and achieve our destiny. We need power to persevere. C. H. Burgen said "Through perseverance, the snail reached the ark." What is an oak tree? It's a small acorn that would not give up its ground Do you want power to stay with it and not give up?

How many would like to have joy in your life? Nehemiah tells us that the joy of the Lord is your strength (Nehemiah 8:10). But sometimes we are just grouchy.

How many would like patience in your life? I mean patience that enables you to put up with people who are getting on your last nerve. And some people, it just seems that their mission in life is to provoke you.

A man went to this diner every Saturday morning and was always complaining. The cook thought, "I'm going to make it so he can't complain." The man ordered two eggs, one scrabbled and one sunny side up. And the cook said, "I'm going to cook this to perfection. No room for negativity. He won't have any reason to be ugly here." The cook worked hard on it and personally presented the eggs to the man and they were gorgeous. The man looked up and said, "You scrambled the wrong egg" Do you feel like you sometimes need patience?

How many would like to have purity and integrity in your life? There are a lot of temptations out there. You feel pressure to compromise and conform to the standards of the world. You may say, "I thought you don't struggle with sin anymore once you get saved." But that's when you really start your struggle with sin! Before you got saved, you just gave into it. Now you are opposing it. You don't know how strong a wind is if you just go down into the shelter to hide yourself and lay down. But you know how strong the currents of wind are when you are out in the open marching against it. But in the middle of this pressure, we are called upon to conform to the image of Christ. How many of you would like to have purity and integrity in your life?

Alright! I guess you are responding in the affirmative: "I want love, I want power, I want patience, I want joy, I want integrity, I want it all these things" These are actually trick questions.

"Blessed be *the God and Father of our Lord Jesus Christ, who has blessed us with every spiritual blessing in the heavenly* places *in Christ."* – *Ephesians 1:3*

If you are a Christian, you already have these things in your life. You have all the resources you need. They are already resident inside of you.

"as His divine power has given to us all things that pertain to life and godliness through the knowledge of him who called us by glory and virtue." – *2 Peter 1:3*

I want you to notice the past tense in both those verses. Both Paul and Peter agree this is past tense. You have already been blessed with every spiritual blessing in Christ Jesus. All these blessings are in Christ. Do you have Christ? All these blessings are in Him. Peter says you have all things that pertain to life and to godliness. It's already yours -you have it. You may say, "Yes, logically yes, theoretically yes, potentially yes; but even though I have these things, I don't have them." So the question for us is this, "How do I release my resources?" The Bible story before us answers this question with exciting narrative.

A Family that Seemed Forsaken

When I was 16 year of age, I went to Lee University. Mom and Dad drove me those 10 hours down 81 South and we got to Cleveland, Tennessee. We found my dorm room -Walker Hall. We were so pumped up. I was starting my career in the ministry. This was my preparation. I went there single. Most singles who go to Bible school want a Mr. Degree or a Mrs. Degree. They are very interested in finding a help mate for ministry. Some of the students come to Bible college already married. The married students weren't in the same dorms with all of the single lonely students.

I noticed how excited these newlyweds were as they launched into an educational journey to lead them to ministerial leadership. They had all these dreams and visions of starting a church together or taking a church that was already in existence and taking it to another level. Some had ambitions of going out to the mission field to make an impact on culture and the Kingdom of God. They felt they had a call of God upon their lives, and they were there to study and to apply themselves. Such joy and vision these young couples had!

That is what it was with this one dear lady, the widow in 2 Kings. Her husband, felt the call of God on his life. He was a righteous man. He was a man who feared God. They were in the Bible school of ministry under the prophet Elijah. Elijah was the president of this Bible school. They were learning to prophesy and bring spiritual revival to the nation. It was an exciting place to be. But then something happened— this Bible student died. I don't know if he was a freshman or a sophomore. I don't know if he was a graduate student or undergraduate. But suddenly he died.

Can you imagine a man who feared God and had the call of God on his life and all of a sudden his life is cut short? I don't know what happened. Did he have a lingering disease? Did he have a stabbing heart attack and shocked everybody with his collapse? Was there an accident? There were bible students cutting down trees for facility enlargement projects; did a tree fall on his head? We're not sure, but he died and it was a shocking tragedy for his dear wife.

In those days, there were no Social Security benefits or insurance plans to assist. Everything was gone! That's the sense of the Scripture. Elijah asked, "What is in you house?" She said "Nothing." I suppose they had already come for the stove and the refrigerator. They had already come for the chairs, sofa and the bed. That house was cleaned out because of debt.

God never forsakes his people. But sometimes things happen to us where it feels like we are forsaken by God. This woman cried out in distress, and now the creditors were coming to take the boys. How long would they be in a position of servitude to satisfy the debt? Perhaps she would never see them again. This mother was heartbroken. She lost her husband and now the two boys were forced into a kind of enslavement. This was a family that seemed forsaken.

A Flask that was Forgotten

The prophet Elijah, the president of the Bible school, showed up and he met with this dear lady. He represented God. He directly asked her, "What do need? What do you want? What do you want me to do for you?" She was invited to make her petition known to God. This is when our resources are set in motion for dispatch. It is prayer that unlocks the door and opens up the storehouses of heaven.

Then Elijah had another question for the widow. He said, "What do you have? What do you have in your house?" She answered, "Nothing! Look around preacher, they have taken everything. This house is vacant. All is gone. We don't have a bed to sleep in. We don't have anything. Oh - well, We have this little jar of oil." Her answer reveals that she thought very little of the jar. She treated it as if it were nothing!

This oil that she possessed should not have been slighted. It was not Wesson oil, 3M oil or coal oil that's used for lighting lanterns. It was sanctified oil! It was a sacred object. The Hebrew word for oil is "anointing." They would take six quarts of oil and mix it with special ingredients using a variety of spices and fragrances and then the consecrated oil would be placed on the head of a man being ordained for the work of prophet, priest or king. This was oil that was placed on her husband's head for him to be a prophet of God. This was the only thing she had left of her husband's ministry, but she didn't seem to really understand or reverence the significance of that.

In the Bible, the oil symbolizes the power and the presence of the Holy Spirit. Often we don't respect the presence of the Spirit in our lives. God has to come in and reduce us down to nothing to show us that if we have the presence of the Spirit, then we have everything we need. Oh, we can get so attached to temporal earthly things, and try to depend on ourselves. We can trust in our achievements and our accumulations, but often our lives become so cluttered that they eclipse God.

Christians in the church at Corinth seemed to have lost their sense of appreciation for the presence of the Spirit in their lives. They were riddled with division and defeat along with confusion and carnality. Paul wrote to remind them of the treasure they possessed through the indwelling Holy Spirit, "Don't you know that your body is the temple of the Holy Spirit who is in you? (1 Corinthians 6:19)

We need to get to the place where we know that if we have the Spirit of God in our lives, we have all that we need to succeed and to be strong.

- ➢ You may not have Coca Cola! But that's alright, Christ is the real thing.

- ➢ You may not have a bottle of Bayer aspirin! But that's alright, He works wonders.

- ➢ You may not have General Electric! But that's ok, because He brings good things to life.

- ➢ You may not have Tide detergent! But that's alright for He gets every last stain out!

- ➢ You may not have Allstate Insurance! But that's quite alright, with Him you are always in good hands!

- ➢ You may not have a Hallmark greeting card! But that's alright too! He cares enough to send the best.

- ➤ You may not have a little tube of Rolaids! But that's alright, He gives 100% relief!

- ➤ You may not have State Farm Insurance! But that's alright, He's a neighbor that will always be there.

- ➤ You may have no Maxwell coffee! But that's all right, taste and see the Lord is good to the very last drop!

- ➤ You may not have a bowl of Frosted Flakes! But that's all right! Because He is always grrreat!

God will appoint trials to come into our lives so that all the trash and trivia are removed and we are reduced to just a bottle of oil. Then we will discover the sufficiency of the presence of God in our lives.

A Faith that Learned to Function

A bottle of oil is sufficient, but that oil must be activated and applied. It can't stay in the jar. What is that oil doing for you? The prophet Elijah gave this woman some instruction, "Go and gather as many vessels as you possible can." This required a real step of faith.

It's hard to define faith. Faith is easier to describe than to define, because faith is being responsive to the Word of God. God will always give you an assignment. He will always give you an activity. Faith says, "Yes Lord, I'm going to follow your lead and I'm going to do what you are telling me to do!"

When God determines to do a miracle, He often demands the muscle of faith to be exercised. Have you ever seen that pattern in the Scripture?

You see it when Jesus raised Lazarus from the dead. If Jesus had the power to raise a man from the dead who had been dead for four days and his body was now decomposed, don't you think He had the power to just speak to that big bolder that was in front of that cave and make it disappear? He said to those standing by "Roll away the stone."

They argued and debated and that is what we will be tempted to do when the Lord gives us instructions. "It doesn't make sense Lord, it sounds stupid." Martha protested, "but his body is stinking now. Don't embarrass us, we want to preserve some dignity after the funeral." In spite of the resistance to His command, they rolled away the stone. Then Jesus manifested His resurrection power and raised Lazarus from the dead.

Do you think that if Jesus had the power to turn water into wine, He had the power to put water in those jugs? If Jesus had the power to transform H2O into high quality merlot, don't you think Jesus had the power to go to simply speak to six empty jars and replenish them with water? But He chose not to do it that way. He told the servants fill up the water jugs. They might have questioned the validity of their assignment. Then I imagine they really struggled with the task of drawing water of out those containers and serving the governor a water beverage, but they did as the Lord commanded. As they drew water out of those six jugs, a miracle took place and the water was turned into wine.

This dear widow with oil, she was given an assignment from God. God said, "Go into the neighborhood, knock on doors and ask people to share with you their pots and pans." Her faith was activated as she simply obeyed the command of the prophet.

A Flow that did not Fail

The two sons went all through the neighborhood and gathered together vessels of every shape and size. All kind of containers and jars were piled up in that empty house. They shut the door following the instructions of the Lord. I don't know if they were excited about what they were doing. They probably thought this was kind of silly.

The first son brought a pot and it was probably wide and deep. Mother thought, "Oh well, we have just a little flask of oil. I guess we will not fill this vessel up very much." She began to pour, and the oil kept coming out and it filled up that pot. And then she said to the brother, "Bring me another pot," He went to the stash and selected a vessel. She lifted up the jar of oil and said, "Let's try it again." She tipped over the jar and that filled up that vessel. The son probably sighed, "That is all we are going to get out of that. It's amazing we got that much out of that flask, but I think we are done." She said, "No, bring me another vessel." They brought another vessel, she poured out the oil and, to the amazement of all three, completely filled that container.

Now they were really excited. She said, "Bring me another vessel." They got into a party spirit in which they were tossing vessels to mother and she was pouring in the oil. The assembly line was working fast and they were astonished at the provision that never ran dry. And then the excitement was over! Suddenly, the oil stopped flowing. When they ran out of empty vessels they could not squeeze another drop out of that jar of oil.

That's why the prophet Elijah had said, "Don't gather just a few vessels." Often our faith is too small! We limit God and His blessings! When the pouring party was over, the family was instructed to sell the containers of oil. With that sale they were able to pay off their debts and secure their future.

God is greater than our sorrows, debts, set-backs and perplexities. God is unlimited in His resources to supply our needs and sufficiently save our souls. He demands that we have faith to respond in a positive way to His Word.

I remember when I took my first church in Laurel, Maryland. I had been to Bible school and had completed a lot of study, but still I didn't feel ready for this challenge. I was only 25 years of age when I took this little church. It was my responsibility to preach three times a week as well as give pastoral care to the congregation. I was overwhelmed with the task of writing three new sermons a week.

I would empty myself out on Sundays and limp back to the parsonage late Sunday with the dread of getting ready for three more sermons for the following week. I would go home and say, "Lord, what am I going to say next week? I can't think of anything else to share. I've preached today everything from Genesis to Revelation. I guess next Sunday I'll be in the maps of the Bible and back in the glossary. I told every story I know. I've shared every testimony I've got. I've told every joke I know. I tried to be inspiring but I am now empty. I have nothing else to give. What am I going deliver to the people in the coming week? I want them to be edified and strengthened. They have expectations for the shepherd to feed them. Will I let them down? God, I want to be a good pastor and bless your people. But I feel so dry and depleted. "

Here is my testimony! God never once failed me! On Monday morning I would rise up and get back to work. Throughout the week I functioned as a Pastor and each week I discovered something wonderful. As I would read, pray and fulfill my duties – the oil began to flow and I found myself being re-filled.

Sure enough, the next Sunday there was always something fresh and inspirational that met the needs of the hour. There was always something powerful and relevant from the pulpit and the congregation would be satisfied. During my pastorate at Laurel I preached 523 sermons and it seemed like every message was fresh manna from heaven. It built a great church and God did wondrous things.

When you step out in faith and pour yourself into empty vessels, you are going to discover there is a flow that will not fail. Your cup will overflow and you can release your resources.

Recently our church sponsored a trip to Niagara Falls. The roar of water going over the edge and crashing to the rocks below was amazing. Did you know that 600,000 gallons go over the falls every second? That is 1 million bathtubs full of water every minute. One day in February of 1848, the falls were cut off. People were looking at the falls and all of a sudden, it went silent and there was no water. An investigation discovered that there were blocks of ice which formed north of the Falls and stopped the flow of the river.

I got to thinking to myself, "God is such a God of abundance. He gives more than enough but sometimes the Falls, the cascade of God's loving kindness, is just cut off. Why is this?" Because blocks of ice form in our lives and dam up the flow. Ice blocks of unbelief and inactivity will stop the flow of divine blessings. The frozen glaciers of despair and discouragement will hinder the generous flow of divine favor. We can release the resources that God has deposited within us if we will live by faith.

A DELIVERANCE CHURCH

John 8:31

Then Jesus said to those Jews who believed Him, "If you abide in My word, you are My disciples indeed. And you shall know the truth, and the truth shall make you free." They answered Him, "We are Abraham's descendants, and have never been in bondage to anyone. How *can* You say, 'You will be made free'?" Jesus answered them, "Most assuredly, I say to you, whoever commits sin is a slave of sin. And a slave does not abide in the house forever, *but* a son abides forever. Therefore if the Son makes you free, you shall be free indeed.

Mrs. Bird was a wonderful children's church director, and one Sunday morning she was sponsoring a children's pageantry. It was a reenactment of Creation. Little six-year-old Jonathan loved his part. He was playing God. His job was to climb the ladder with a flashlight and when he heard the words, "Let there be light," he was to turn on the flashlight and shine it upon the activities on the stage. Mrs. Bird was on the stage getting everybody in order. Some of the children were fish, some were animals, and some were trees. Suddenly, she felt a tug on her skirt. She turned around and there was Jonathan. He didn't look happy. He said, "Mrs. Bird, can you find someone else today to play my part? I just feel too crazy to be God today."

Our lives are crazy if we ignore God or if we try to be God. Sometimes we think we can manage our lives with our own wisdom and resources. What a relief it is to climb down from that lofty ladder and say, "You know, I'm feeling too crazy to be God today." The beginning of deliverance, healing, and recovery is humility. Pride is the enemy of hope.

I'm inspired thinking about Bill W. It was 80 years ago he was addicted to alcohol. His life was a mess. He couldn't keep a job, and four times he was in the hospital desperate and losing his health. He had to be put in prison because of his addiction. The doctor said to his wife, "Louise, you have three options; you can lock him up, you can watch him go insane, or you can just let him die." Bill W. was hopeless and desperate. He hit rock bottom but he stumbled into a church called Calvary Church in New York City. In that church there was a little group called the Oxford group. They were all about honesty, compassion, prayer and a simple focus on the Lord Jesus Christ. In that fellowship, Bill W. was delivered. Out of that deliverance Alcoholics Anonymous was born. We thank God for that movement and that ministry. It has been instrumental for more than eight decades to empower people to live lives of responsibility, sobriety and freedom. They used the Bible or the "Big Book" to develop the 12 step program.

There is freedom in the Lord Jesus Christ. We find deliverance when we take deliberate steps to follow after Jesus Christ. Following Jesus involves an immersion into the Bible. Jesus said, "You will know the truth and the truth will set you free" (john 8:32). Deliverance from any addictive behavior is important. Addictive behavior is destructive to ourselves and to others. Because of addictions there are wrecked marriages, broken families, shattered hearts, and ruined reputations. But we proclaim again that there is deliverance in the Lord Jesus Christ.

Rather than cover the 12 steps in this chapter, we will roll those steps into 3 essential steps and consider God's path for deliverance and freedom.

Get Real

Maybe this first step is a surprise. Some have the idea that deliverance starts with high motivation for self-improvement through increased self-esteem. But the road to recovery does not start with a purchase of self-help books and a determination to do better. Trying harder will just make you fall harder. The first step is a way of *humility*.

The starting step in the AA program goes like this, "We admit we are powerless over our fatal attraction and our lives have become unmanageable." Here is the honesty and humility that we need to get on the path of deliverance. Confession of sin may seem old-fashion, but this is the Bible way (I John 1:9).

We resist labeling our wrong behavior as sin and we would rather call our bad behavior a disease or an error in judgment. The Bible talks about sin in our lives. Sin is not a very popular word today. In fact, it's kind of funny, because today the only time you see the word sin is on a dessert menu at a restaurant. I came across an article about a new restaurant called "Zen and Sin." The advertisement read, "A reservation only deserves space for savory 20 decadent dishes and sipping champagne cocktails and fine wine." I'm not against this restaurant. In fact, I'm kind of hesitant to mention it because this might be the only thing you remember of the sermon. I know you're going to get on the parking lot and go "What was the name of that restaurant that pastor was recommending?"

Our problem is a sin problem and God provides an answer for our sinful situation. "If we confess our sins, He is faithful and just to forgive us our sins and to cleanse us from all unrighteousness" (I John 1:9). We are all in the same category when it comes to being sinners- even though sin is manifested in different ways. We must put away our pious masks, confess our sinful nature, face our struggle and claim the pardon and purging that only God can give.

We need to be a "me too" church. I'm not talking about you getting in the lobby of the church and you ask another attender how he is doing and he says, "I am doing fantastic! The kids are overachieving, the fish are jumping, the cobs are high, daddy is rich and mama is good looking," and you say, "Me too." That's not the context for the "me too" that I'm talking about. I'm talking about something else. When you're in the lobby and someone says to you, "I make a mess of things." And you say, "Me too." That is the kind of humble posture each Christian should maintain.

In fact, I want us to practice this. This needs to be part of our atmosphere and part of our liturgy. So let's try this out!

Here is my confession:

> "Left to myself, I waste my one and only life in a thousand stupid ways." And the congregation says, "Me too."

> "Left to myself, I make an idol of my success and my image." And the congregation says, "Me too."

> "Left to myself, I dishonor my sexuality." And the congregation says, "Me too."

> "Left to myself, I use my words to deceive and destroy people instead of edifying them." And the congregation says, ,"Me too."

> "Left to myself, instead of serving people out of love, I use people for my own advancement." And the congregation says, "Me too."

> "Left to myself, greed rules my wallet." And the congregation says, "Me too."

> "Left to myself, resentment fills my heart in nano second." And the congregation says, "Me too."

> "Left to myself, pride governs my choices." And the congregation says, "Me too."

Wasn't that fun and freeing? Let's be a "Me too" church. This is the kind of atmosphere that will promote and make possible personal deliverance.

I was reading an article where a dear man named Jim was at his Tuesday night AA meeting in the basement of a church. He had been in the program for many years now and was enjoying a testimony of being clean. Each week He would get up and say, "My name is Jim, I'm an alcoholic." Then he would ask for help.

On this particular night, a new fellow came in with a crisp suit and paraded in with a swagger. When he stood up to identify himself, he wouldn't even admit he was an alcoholic. He kind of stumbled around trying to talk about his struggle without saying it. Then he blamed other people and said he was a victim. Jim with dreadlocks and dark shades sitting in the back, kind of smiled, laughed and then leaned over to his buddy and whispered in his ear, "Oh that is pitiful. I use to feel that way before I achieved low self-esteem."

The only way to go up is to come down. There's only one way for deliverance and that is to be brutally honest, confess sin to God, take responsibility for actions, and cast oneself onto the rich mercy of God.

Get Help

To get deliverance we must get help. Now that is the hope that AA gives to people- that you don't have to stay stuck. You don't have to remain in your chains. There is a higher power. Through the years, many have felt they had to be vague about a higher power. But I want to declare to you that the higher power is the Lord Jesus Christ.

Pam was raised in a family that caused her so much pain, she was driven to drink. She chose to be a drunkard and at the age of 20. She would brag that she could drink any guy under the table. But her life was a train wreck, cycling in and out of marriages! She got desperate and began to attend AA meetings, but she couldn't really get into this higher power thing. She couldn't really turn to God because her mother was of one religion and her father was from another religion, and they fought over that. So she saw the friction related to God.

At a young age she was turned off to all ideas of church, spirituality and God. But she liked this idea of a higher power because she needed something outside of herself to change her. But she really didn't know with whom to connect. She thought, "How do I define a higher power?"

Randomly she decided to call her higher power Ralph.

She was doing okay with AA and Ralph as her high power, but there was still a lot of frustration and defeat in her journey because the higher power was too fictional Then one day, a man came stumbling into the Tuesday night basement meeting. He was not smelling well and his appearance was ragged. He stood up and said, "My name is Ralph." And before he could say anything else, he puked all over the floor.

Pam was sitting there and her heart was pierced. She said, "I don't need Ralph to be my higher power." The next day she went to her Christian beautician Kathy. While getting her hair done, Kathy begin to discern that something was wrong, so Kathy began to share her faith with Pam. That is exactly what Pam needed. Pam began to attend a Bible study where she learned about the true higher power, the Lord Jesus Christ. That's when full deliverance came to her life.

We all are slaves to Satan and sin prior to the miracle of regeneration. We cannot free ourselves and sometimes we don't want to admit that. When Jesus announced this universal enslavement, His audience began to argue because they were thinking in terms of political oppression. They boasted that they had never been enslaved since they were the descendants of Abraham. Of course, that was not an honest assessment of their national history.

Did they forget about Babylon? Did they forget about Rome that was now oppressing them? Jesus answered, "You have been in political bondage for years. But worse than that, if you commit sin then you are a slave to sin. You are in spiritual bondage and the slave doesn't stay in the house. The slave does not enjoy residence in the home of the master and cannot face the future with confidence and hope. But If the Son shall set you free, you shall be free indeed. Slavery will end and you will become a beloved child of God who remains in the house" (my free paraphrase of John 8:34-36).

True freedom! The Son sets us free! Christ delivers from the condemnation of sin. The guilt is gone! Then He comes and delivers us from the control of Satan, breaking the authority of evil that captivates the human heart. Christ adopts us into the family of God in which we enjoy a permanent status as children of the Most High God. David's confidence becomes our confidence, "Surely goodness and mercy shall follow me all the days of my life and I will dwell in the House of the Lord forever" (Psalms 23:6).

The goodness of God's pursues us each day so that we receive His provisions. His mercy pursues us each day so that we enjoy His pardon and then this assurance of eternal life anchors us in hope – we know we will dwell forever in the Father's house. With this confidence reigning in our hearts, we are able to face every sinful habit with faith and grace. As Christians, we do not fight for victory; we fight from victory.

Get Up

Our faith is not passive, it's an active faith. John 5 narrates the wonderful story of how Jesus went to the pool of Bethesda where a man had been suffering for 38 years. He was in an immobile situation. He had no strength in his body and he had nobody to help him. Jesus said to him, "Rise. Pick up your bed and walk. Get up."

The call of God summons us to take action. He demands that we participate in His power, with His people, in His house, and according to His purposes. Don't stay where you are! Don't accept where you are! Get up!

A group of psychologists did some experiments in the 1970s in which they put a fat rat in a cage with two bottles of water. One bottle contained pure H_2O and the other was water laced with heroin. Every time they conducted the experiment, it was the same situation. The rat would drink from both bottles, but get attached to the bad water and then self-destruct.

Then researchers did something else. Instead of using a single rat cage, they built a large cage that accommodated many rats. It was like a luxury, deluxe park for rats. It included toys, tunnels, spinning wheels and lots of good food. The cage still included the same two bottles - a bottle of pure water and a bottle laced with heroin. All the rats sampled both bottles.

In that cage called the Rat Park, not one rat drank twice from the poisoned water. They just drank once, left it, and drank from the pure water and never did self-destruct. In a community of rats, the individual rats were empowered to make the right choices concerning the bottles.

Isolation will destroy you! Inactivity will destroy you! Self-pity will destroy you! You must get up! God has a place for you, it is called the Rat Park (the church). Hang out with some other rats. We're all sinners. We're all in the same condition of addictive behavior and besetting sins. However, the community of believers will empower us.

In the fellowship of Christians we are built up with **affirmation**. In the Rat Park (church) our true identity as "overcomers" is celebrated. People remember the sign of the covenant that was sealed in water baptism. We are invited to the Lord's Table to remember that Christ was given for us. We hear the ministry of the Word which proclaims all God's promises that anchor us in the truth of what God says about us.

Out of that sense of Christian identity we are able to fight the good fight of faith and experience a release of His divine power at work within us.

In the fellowship of Christians we are protected with **accountability.** We need the authority of Bible teaching and spiritual leadership to challenge the indulgences of the ego and the flesh. "But exhort one another daily, while it is called 'Today,' lest any of you be hardened through the deceitfulness of sin" (Hebrews 3:13).

In the fellowship of Christians we benefit with **appropriation.** What a transformation takes place in lives when we partake of the glory of God. We participate in the divine nature through Scripture, sacraments, songs, prayers and praise. Paul tells us that a face to face experience with the glory of God will be a metamorphosis in which we will be changed into the likeness of Christ (II Corinthians 3:16-18).

If you want to take the bone away from a bulldog, you know how to do it? You don't wrestle that bone away from that dog. He will bite you. No, you give him a big T-bone steak, and he will leave that bone. How do we walk away from the dry bones that the devil throws at us? We replace those dry bones with the big juicy steaks God offers to us. A spiritual feast will reduce our carnal appetite!

In the fellowship of Christians we get connected with **activity.** I didn't tell you one little piece of the puzzle of how AA got started. Bill W. found deliverance through Jesus Christ at the Oxford group. He was doing well but he was on a business trip in Akron, Ohio. It was the day before Mother's Day, and years before, his mother had deserted him. So he was feeling, angry, bitter, lonely, and self-pity.

He was in the lobby of the hotel and there was a bar at the other end and he got thirsty. He had been sober for a while, trusting in Christ, but now it was a battle, he felt fragile. "Oh Lord, I'm going to drink, I'm going to go back to that bondage." Then a thought came to him. I've got to find another alcoholic." He looked up a local church, talked to the pastor and found in that community an alcoholic. His name was Dr. Bob.

Bill W. took him to lunch and. began to share with Dr. Bob his journey; his deliverance. At that lunch, Dr. Bob got saved and delivered. And it was at that luncheon that those two men together formulated AA and came up with the Big Book and the 12 steps. A crucial part in recovery is this- if you want to stay victorious, you've got to help somebody else get to victory. Bill W. wasn't just thinking out of compassion, "I've got to save a drunk." He was thinking, "I'm going to get drunk if I don't save a drunk. I've got to share my story. I've got to get busy being used of God. I can't keep this to myself."

When we get involved in the calling of God and begin to serve others, we become less self-absorbed. All of a sudden we have the joy of being used of God. We sense the anointing of the Spirit flowing through us and that becomes a greater "high" than any drug or drink.

A Liturgical Church

I Corinthians 14:39-40

Therefore, brethren, desire earnestly to prophesy, and do not forbid to speak with tongues. Let all things be done decently and in order.

I have been collecting names of churches that I find interesting:

- My Brother is a Christian Church of God

- Satan is in Trouble Ministries

- Devil Go Home, Here I Am Jesus Ministry

- Jesus the Landlord, We the Relaxing Pew Ministries

- Trigger Happy Ministry – Always Firing at the Devil

- The Cowboy Church – Rounding up Souls for Jesus

- Flipping Church of God

- Praise All Day Church of the Redeemer Christ our Everlasting King(must cost a fortune to put those words on the church van)

- Hell Hole Swamp Baptist Church (named after a town in South Carolina)

- Calvin Freewill Baptist Church (a very confused church)

- Boring Seventh-day Adventist Church (it is interesting to note that the name of the pastor is Reverend Dull)

- ➤ The Exciting Singing Hills Baptist Church

- ➤ Scum of Sinners Bible Chapel

- ➤ Big Ugly Free Will Baptist Church (name of the town in West Virginia)

- ➤ Little Hope Baptist Church (not very encouraging, but definitely better than No Hope Methodist Church)

- ➤ Vatican Baptist Church (also confused)

Names of churches are important because they have the power to appeal to the community and they convey something about the kind of worship that takes place in the sanctuary. It is good if a church claims to be liturgical! The word *liturgy* communicates a special order of worship that respects Scripture, honors tradition and dignifies worship.

So what is liturgy? Liturgy is a system of public worship in the Christian Church. Every church has a liturgy (whether they admit it or not).

I was raised in a fellowship in which we boasted that we were not a liturgical church, and yet we had a very precise and predictable pattern of worship.

It is true that some forms of worship are more formal and traditional than others, but in its most basic definition the subject of liturgy is a reference to a form of worship that each church embraces. In its more technical meaning, liturgy is a form of worship that is based on the Bible, rooted in hundreds of years of tradition, and outlined by the common book of prayer or directed by another ecclesiastical book that prescribes worship for the universal church.

The church I have the honor of leading, Calvary Gospel Church, is what I call "liturgy lite." Not "Miller Lite," but "liturgy lite." We take many of the traditional forms of worship and incorporate them into our Sunday experience, but we do not use them all (e.g. we do not wear robes for preaching, use incense, set up a bishop's chair).

Our style of worship is actually called *convergence worship,* which combines the three main streams of modern Christian worship: evangelical, charismatic, and liturgical. *Evangelical* is a category of worship that emphasizes strong Bible preaching. *Charismatic* is a category of worship that emphasizes the manifestation of the gifts of the Spirit. *Liturgical* is a category of worship that emphasizes a formal-traditional set program.

Here at Calvary, we have all three streams flowing into one mighty river of worship. We are an *evangelical* church with the pulpit as the center piece announcing preaching as the core activity of worship. We are *charismatic*, embracing the gifts of the Spirit and praying for their supernatural expressions. We are *liturgical* with a strong commitment to traditional Christianity. What a grand idea! Convergence worship—three streams, but one river.

Let's focus in on the three main considerations regarding liturgy:

1. God Supports Ardor and Order

2. God Sanctifies Sight and Sound

3. God Saturates the Ordinary

God Supports Ardor and Order

Every church has to deal with this order-ardor tension. We all love ardor— fire, zeal, enthusiasm, free expression and spontaneity!

But we also love order—structure, dignity, and form. Where is the balance between the two?

Churches often tend to gravitate towards extremes. Some churches emphasize a proper sense of order, but the atmosphere becomes suffocating— dryer than cracker juice! They have sound doctrine, but everyone is sound asleep! Other churches veer towards the opposite extreme-ardor. They are filled with fire, but it is a destructive wildfire! They create a lot of noise, but the noise is void of any clearly communicated content (my grandmother used to say that the empty barrels make the most noise).

An Episcopalian was talking with a Pentecostal brother, and they did not see things alike. The Pentecostal thought the Episcopalian was boring and unspiritual. The Pentecostal said, "Oh, your services are so dry and routine. All that formality! It gives me the chills. You know, a body without the spirit is a corpse." The Episcopalian replied, "Yes, I know that's a danger, but also remember—a spirit without a body is a spook!"

We need a middle ground here. Our Sunday bulletin each week outlines a specific form of worship. At the end of the program there is a small disclaimer attached: "Program subject to change depending on the leading of the Spirit."

One Wednesday night, the Spirit of God was flowing in a special way through a choir song, so we asked the choir to repeat the song while people came forward for prayer. That was not in the program, nor did we plan or anticipate that event! Nonetheless, that is what God wanted.

When it comes to worship, we must have flexibility and spiritual sensitivity. We read in the Old Testament that the glory-cloud filled the temple with such holy presence that the ministers could not minister! On that occasion, the priests were unable to perform their normal duties because the presence of God had so saturated the house.

There will be times we have to throw our program out the window because the presence of God is filling and thrilling in such an unusual way. Most of the time, however, the Spirit of God will work through the program He helped us create. He will animate the liturgy and anoint the activities of worship so that nothing becomes boring or ritualistic. God supports both order and ardor.

God Sanctifies Sight and Sound

In Lancaster, Pennsylvania., there is a Christian theatre called "Sight and

Sound" which specializes in Bible-based dramas. They incorporate music, lighting, elaborate staging, and costumes to create a truly unique worship experience. (I also enjoy the smell of hot almonds in the lobby). Every worship experience should be a drama and every sanctuary should be called "Sight and Sound." Each Sunday, there should be elements of worship that appeal to all five senses. After all, did not God become flesh and dwell among us? Jesus invited His disciples to touch, feel, see, and hear His presence.

In my college career, I focused on the field of education, and the instructors drilled it into me that there are different kinds of learners. Some are audio learners who learn by hearing. Some are visual learners who learn by seeing. Some are kinetic learners who learn by touching and doing. In fact, most of us are a combination of these. Statistics show that people remember ten percent of what they hear, thirty percent of what they see, and eighty percent of what they do. Since God created us to be seers, hearers, and doers, He also provides us with a form of worship that engages all five senses—a total worship experience for the total being.

Sight

We see the special colors of fabric and candles that reflect seasonal themes. We see the processional that jump-starts the worship. We see the banners that express truth. We see the dance and robed chair.

Smell

During worship we smell things. The burning candle gives us sense of the fragrant presence of the Holy Spirit who illuminates the Word of God. The Old Testament Temple was filled with holy perfume that made the presence of God much more precious.

Touch

We feel things during worship. The holy oil on the brow is applied when praying for the sick and helps the seeker to sense the power of the Holy Spirit. The holy kiss is gently placed on the cheek in times of fellowship to give tangible expression of love.

Sound

During worship we hear things. Oh, he that has ears let him hear what the Spirit says to the churches! We hear music! We hear preaching and teaching! We hear testimonies! We hear Bible readings!

Taste

We taste things as we worship. The bread and the wine of the Eucharist is placed in the mouth to provide a physical communion with the living Christ. We taste the honey of the Word of God as we speak it in responsive Bible reading. We taste the goodness of the Lord as we use our tongues to sing of His praises.

Worship excites all the senses, plugging us into a holy encounter with God. Worship is action. In fact, the root definition for liturgy means "The work of the people." There is a set program of worship to ensure that people come to church as participators, not spectators.

We tend to misunderstand Sunday worship. We see a stage with a choir and preacher on the stage and then congregants filling the pews. We come to the conclusion that the congregation is the audience while those on stage are performers and entertainers. The congregation becomes a group of consumers and spectators. But this should not be! The entire sanctuary is a stage and God is the audience! We each have a script with a part to play. When we make our exodus from the sanctuary, we should not be asking each other, "Did you enjoy the service? Did you get anything out of it?" No! We should bow and ask God, "Did you enjoy the service? Did you get anything out of it?"

Liturgy is the corporate and unified gift that we present to our God on Sunday mornings. As we each play our part, we harmonize with others and give to God a lovely bouquet of flowers—a gorgeous demonstration of spiritual gifts arranged in a decent order of reverence and adoration. We do not come here to do our own thing, that would be chaos.

When I was in high school, I joined the marching band. On Saturdays, we performed on the football field at halftime, making wonderful designs on the field. Each band player had a specific place to walk, and it was imperative that each member of the band followed the plan. The band spelled out words and formed images on the field that could be seen from the stands.

One Saturday afternoon, I was on the field with the band and I was playing my trumpet. I got lost in the song and forgot my part. We were all marching toward the end-zone and when we came to the twenty yard line, the entire group made a quick pivot, turning around to march toward the opposite end-zone. I guess I was enjoying tooting my own horn, because I forgot to turn. Finally, I looked up from the little song book that was attached to the end of my trumpet to find that I was marching in the wrong end-zone all by myself! The entire group was on the other side of the field.

Some people treat worship that way! They forget about the script, indulging in private worship that shows no regard for the disciplines of corporate worship. While the entire congregation collectively presents a wonderful gift of praise to God, one person stands in the opposite end-zone tooting his own horn. Liturgy creates a unity so that we can worship God as a unified fellowship

---

Psalm 133: 1-3

Behold, how good and how pleasant it is for brethren to dwell together in unity. It is like the oil upon the head, running down on the beard, the beard of Aaron. Running down the edge of his garments. It is like the dew of Hermon, descending upon the mountains of Zion; for there the Lord commanded blessings — Life evermore.

God Saturates the Ordinary

Sometimes God will work in an unusual manner. He will surprise us with a glorious manifestation and a new method, and we ought to be open to such possibilities. I was not negative concerning the five-year revival that took place in Pensacola, Florida, with its unusual expressions. I was not negative concerning the laughing revival of Toronto— people would travel up there and come back laughing their heads off for Jesus! One recent revival involved jerking. That is fine! I am very open to a new and dynamic move of God, because I never want to be guilty of "quenching the Spirit."

At the same time, however, I do not want to disdain the plainness and regularity of the Sunday worship experience. Some people get weary with the Sunday routine—it is too plain, too ordinary, and too ritualistic. I like the way the Westminster Confession describes worship: "God works through the ordinary means of grace: the Word, sacraments, and prayers." I am concerned that the culture of the contemporary church has moved in a direction that makes us restless with holy routine. Think of the vocabulary that is now popular in the church:

• radical	• alternative
• the next level	• innovative
• epic	• the next big
• impactful	thing
• extreme	• on the edge
• emergent	• explosive

Nothing is wrong with this vocabulary, but it makes the word "ordinary" a very lonely word. People begin to disdain the ordinary means of grace as they jump on every band wagon to chase down the latest revival explosion or mystical experience. Constantly yearning for an "extraordinary" manifestation of grace can get exhausting and can lead to disillusionment and disappointment.

The older I get, the more appreciative I become of the "slow and steady" process of spiritual maturity. As we faithfully participate in the ordinary means of grace established by the local church—namely, the Word, sacraments, and prayers— we quietly blossom and develop as Christians. When children are young fishermen, they cannot leave the line in the water long enough to catch anything. To be young is to be restless.

Let us find satisfaction in the simple expression of worship that God ordains for us. Church is not meant to always be sensational or spectacular. Simplicity and regularity in worship are comforting and powerful. Let us acknowledge that every Christian gathering is amazing, awesome, and transformational because it is held in the very presence of God! Jesus said, "Where two or three are gathered in My Name, I am in the midst of them."

A Compassionate Church

Did you know that 20 percent of the population is classified as "Highly Sensitive?" Out of a congregation of 500 people, approximately one hundred of us are HSP's-Highly Sensitive People. Dr. Elain Aron, author of *The Highly Sensitive Person*, describes HSP's as individuals who have an overdeveloped nervous system. Here is a little test from the book to help you determine if you are an HSP:

> ➢ Do you get rattled when you are required to accomplish a lot in a short period of time?

> ➢ Do you make it a high priority to arrange your life to avoid

upsetting and overwhelming situations?

➢ Does the mood of other people greatly affect you?

➢ Are you uncomfortable with loud noises?

➢ Are you deeply moved by art, music, and movies?

➢ Do you startle easily?

➢ Do you often disappear from crowded situations to find some escape and solace?

➢ Do mean internet comments make you sad?

➢ Does it take you ages to make a decision?

➢ Are you a bit of a perfectionist?

➢ Do you hate political arguments?

➢ Do you need a lot of time to decompress?

➢ Do people often say to you, "Don't take things so personally?"

➢ Is it hard for you to say "no" to people?

➢ Does criticism almost cripple you?

➢ Do violent movies greatly disturb you?

➢ Are you a good listener?

➢ Are you extremely polite and well-mannered?

➢ Do you work hard to please other people?

➢ Are you more observant and empathetic to the pain of people around you?

If you have said "yes" to a majority of these questions, then most likely, you are a Highly Sensitive Person. Now, nothing is wrong with that. In fact, I am an HSP (I'm sorry—should I have said that? I hope I didn't offend you. Do you still like me? I hope you do.) In fact, I have a double problem—my nervous system is super sensitive, *and* I am addicted to coffee…. Not a great combination!

Jesus was a sensitive person, but He certainly was not an HSP. He had to fulfill His entire ministry in three short years, and yet it did not rattle Him. He was never in a hurry or out of breath. Furthermore, Jesus did not always come across as polite. Twice we read where He got so angry over the temple being defiled that He took out a whip, drove the money changers away, and knocked over their tables—HSP's do not throw furniture.

Jesus did not feel the need to please everybody. Here was His sermon to one group, "You snakes! You brood of vipers! How will you escape being condemned to hell?" That is not typical HSP language. Often, the presence of Jesus was disturbing and upsetting! He could really irritate people and stir up controversial arguments.

Jesus was not an HSP, but He was full of compassion. In Luke 14, we read about a dinner experience that He had at the home of a prominent Pharisee. At this dinner party, Jesus demonstrated His ability to be controversial and compassionate at the same time. This party was very tense and awkward. Jesus was invited to the dinner for the purpose of being discredited, and He was well aware of this hostile hospitality.

The Bible says that the guests of the dinner "watched" Him, a word that describes staring with malicious intent. Luke uses this same word to describe the sharp watch that the Jews kept on the gates of Damascus when they planned to murder the converted Saul of Tarsus. This was a trap! And once the table was spread, the trap was sprung.

The bait for the trap was a miserable man who was suffering with a disease called dropsy, a painful disease of the liver and kidneys caused by the collection of water in the tissues. This man was hurting. He was brought to the dinner not as a guest, but as a prelude to the party. The Pharisees and religious leaders knew the reputation of Jesus. They knew He could not ignore individuals who were in such a state of misery.

Hoping that Jesus would help the man so that they could criticize Him for violating the Sabbath day rules, they paraded the sick man before

Jesus. The Law of Moses never forbade healing on the Sabbath, but the Jewish society had come up with a rule that no medical treatment could be administered on the Sabbath unless a life was in jeopardy. They wanted Jesus to break this Sabbath day rule so they could pounce on Him.

If Jesus had been an HSP, He would have been tempted to avoid this ugly confrontation. Out of politeness and respect for the man who had invited Him to dinner, He would want to play by the rules and ignore the man with dropsy—look the other way and keep the peace. On the contrary, Jesus was not affable. He asked a question that embarrassed the entire group, "Which of you, having a donkey or an ox that has fallen into a pit, will not immediately pull him out on the Sabbath day?"

Suddenly, there was a long, uncomfortable silence; the Pharisees were tongue tied. They didn't know how to answer. Jesus was rising higher than this foolish debate over Sabbath day rules.

Our society is obsessed with worth. We want to know the worth of *everything!* For example, to discover the worth of a car, just check out the website known as Blue Book… it's called the blue book because when you find out how little your car is worth, you really feel blue! We know the worth of objects, but what is the worth of a human being?

Let's examine the words of Jesus regarding the worth of mankind:

> ➤ *"Look at the birds of the air, they do not sow or reap or store away in barns, and yet your heavenly Father feeds them. Are you not much more valuable than they?"* – Matthew 6:26

> ➤ *"Are not sparrows sold two for a penny? Yet not one of them will fall to the ground outside your Father's care. And even the hairs of your head are all numbered. So don't be afraid; you are worth more than many sparrows."* – Matthew 10:29-31

God values sparrows. He feeds them and gives them trees and twigs for nests. He cares so much for them that He has a running inventory! You, on the other hand, are worth way more than many sparrows. The hairs of your head are all numbered! When you care for someone, you notice details. When a baby is born, what is one of the first things parents do? They look at the fingers and toes and count them. Jesus is saying, "God does not just count your fingers and toes; He loves you so much that He numbers the hairs on your head."

At this party, Jesus created an awkward silence. Maybe the host was thinking, "Well, this dinner is not going too well. My guests are now tongue tied. I hope whoever talks next will pick a safer topic." Jesus talked next, but He did *not* pick a safer topic. He picked a fight. After exposing their heartless religion of legalism, He then proceeded to rebuke their pride and arrogance. "When you are invited to a feast, don't sit down at the best place. If you take the best seat, you might be asked to get up and take a less honorable seat. Take the lowest seat and the only way you can go is up."

Wow! That was not a very nice thing to say at this party. Everyone at this dinner had just finished scrambling for the best seats! The dining room was arranged in a specific order so that it was clear which seat was the most honorable, which seat was the runner up, and which seat was the second runner up in terms of honor. When the cook said, "Soup's on," there was a mad rush to claim the best seat.

Everyone was still out of breath after scrambling to get the best seat, and Jesus rebuked everyone by saying, "Your seating chart is wrong. Not only do you exalt man made rules over the worth of human beings, but you compete with people for status and image. Let me redo your table assignments—exalt somebody else." Now everyone is shifting in their seats and reddening in their faces. The host is thinking, "I invited the wrong person to my house. I hope Jesus doesn't have any more advice."

Of course He did! He turned to the host and said, "Let me tell you something else: when you have a luncheon, don't just invite your friends and family—people who can pay you back with their invitation. In doing this, you simply play round robin with everyone going back and forth enjoying nice dinners at each other's houses. Don't let family and friends be the extent of your social life. Instead, when you put on a luncheon, invite the poor, the crippled, the lame, and the blind. In doing this, you will be blessed. They will not be able to repay you and invite you to their houses, but you will be repaid in the resurrection of the just."

Oh—now the silence around the table was thickened. The host had invited this diseased man to the house not for dinner, but to make him an object of mockery. The man was dismissed before dinner even started. Jesus, on the other hand, wanted to know why the man with dropsy wasn't included on the guest list!

At this point in the party, everybody's blood pressure was off the charts. No one was enjoying the leg of lamb or glass of wine. Somebody at the table was an HSP because he was eager to redeem the dinner and turn the atmosphere into something positive and pleasant. He broke the silence and said, "Blessed is everyone who will eat at the feast in the kingdom of God." This man heard Jesus talk about a feast, and he thought he could make a statement that would unite all the guests and lighten the tension. His tactic did not work; Jesus was on a roll. He would not be distracted and He said, "Let me tell you a story about who is on the guest list for the feast in the kingdom." The host was thinking, "Oh boy, here we go again."

Jesus told the story of a king who sponsored a huge feast and sent out invitations. The invitations, however, did not receive positive responses. People made excuses for not coming to the feast and the king was insulted. Therefore, the king gave orders for the servants to "Go out into the highways and byways. Go into the bad neighborhoods. Go into the slums. Bring in the poor, the maimed, the lame, and the blind. I want my house to be filled." Jesus could not let it go! His message was about compassion. He was so angry that these Pharisees would insult this man with dropsy and use Him as a weapon to discredit a ministry of compassion.

When Jesus was born, a compassion makeover was coming to the world. It was the Christian movement that tenderized the world by creating hospitals, shelters, orphanages, and senior adult centers. The world before Christ was like the Russian tundra—cold and cruel and calloused. Christ introduced charity and benevolence to the world. Let us never be guilty of having the religion of the Pharisees—a heartless legalism, a prideful self-promotion, a good ole boy social club, and an empty house because we don't invite the downtrodden of society. The religion of Jesus is one of compassion.

Saint Laurence was a deacon in the Christian Church who was quite generous, especially to the poor. He lived in Aragon of the Roman empire of the third century. During one of the persecutions, he was ordered to bring to a Roman official some of the treasures of the church, so he went out and returned with what he considered to be the treasures of the church. He brought to the official some individuals who were poor, downtrodden, and lame. The Roman official was insulted, and he had Laurence roasted to death on a gridiron.

Today in Ft. Lauderdale, Florida, there is a shelter for homeless people named after him—Saint Laurence Chapel. This shelter cares for the homeless, offering good meals, a mailbox, job counseling, a shower and bathroom, worship services, and more.

What do we consider the treasures of the church? If you are a HSP like me, do you worry more about social awkwardness than doing the will of God? Oh, that we would show care and compassion to all, even to the least of these.

A BRIDAL CHURCH

A man was invited to an elegant dinner party at the home of an elderly friend. During dinner, the man noticed his friend speaking to his wife with soft, endearing terms, preceding each request with names like "Honey," "Sweetheart," "Darling," or "Pumpkin." Knowing that the couple had been married for over fifty years, the man was quite impressed with their intimacy.

While the wife was in the kitchen, he said to his older friend, "I think it is so wonderful you speak to your wife that way. You have been married for so long, and yet you still call her by all those pet names!"

The old man hung his head and said, "To tell you the truth, about ten years ago I forgot her name and for the life of me cannot remember!"

I hope that as you celebrate each day with your significant other, you employ all of those wonderful pet names—and *not* because you forgot your spouse's real name!

Fortunately, Christ never forgets the name of His bride. He calls us His beloved and He treasures His chosen people. The church is His bride, and so are all its members, together as one and separately. In fact, our names are inscribed within the palms of His hands! Christ loves the church and He gave Himself just for her.

Brides of the Bible

Each bride of the Bible provides us with special insight concerning the mystical union that exists between Christ and His church. The first bride, Eve, serves as a preview to the forming of Christ's bride. God noticed Adam wandering amidst the Garden of Eden. Although he was surrounded by God's glorious creations—beautiful flowers of the fields and majestic fowls of the air—he was alone. Recognizing his loneliness, God said, "It is not good for man to be alone." Therefore, God caused a deep sleep to fall upon Adam (the first anesthesia) and performed surgery upon Adam's side. He then proceeded to remove Adam's rib and, from the rib, He formed a gorgeous creature to be Adam's companion. He must have called her "My prime rib."

Why the side? Why not form Eve from a bone of Adam's head or from a piece of Adam's foot? God refused to use Adam's feet; He did not want Eve to be trampled upon. God declined to use Adam's head; He did not want Eve to be superior to her husband. Instead, God specifically chose a bone from Adam's side so that Eve would be her husband's equal. He removed a bone near Adam's heart so that Eve would be a cherished bride. He pulled a bone that rested beneath the strength of the arm so that Eve would be protected and preserved.

Waking from his sleep, Adam's eyes finally rested upon the crown of God's creation. Adam was so elated, he said, "Woe-man." The name *woman* actually means *man with a womb*.

"Adam, do you love me?" she asked. "Who else?" he replied. There they had a honeymoon in paradise!

In the same manner that God fashioned a wife for Adam, He determined to build a bride for His Son. Unlike Adam, Christ was not lonely. The Godhead is always self-sufficient and self-complete. Wanting to widen the circle of His affection, God chose to build a Bride for Christ simply out of the overflowing plentitude and surplus of His divine love.

Just like Adam, Christ entered a deep sleep—His death on the cross—with His side torn open by the spear of a soldier who had pierced it. From the open wound of this precious side, a gushing flow of blood and water poured upon the ground and from that fountain God formed a bride. Waking early on the first Easter morning, Christ eagerly met with His bride in the Upper Room, speaking "Peace" to her soul and breathing upon her face. The breath of Christ upon His bride—what sweeter kiss could ever be found! Fifty days later, on the Day of Pentecost, Christ fully animated His bride by sending the promised Holy Spirit.

Through the power of the Spirit the church enjoys a reciprocal indwelling with Christ and actually experiences union with Him. He lovingly looks upon His bride with words of admiration and affirmation, "You are now bone of my bone, flesh of my flesh." There is no greater bond in heaven or earth than the bond that exists between Christ and His bride—the union we enjoy with Him is beyond comprehension!

The story of another biblical bride, Rebekah, demonstrates the role that the Holy Spirit plays in God's pursuit of a bride for His Son. Father Abraham wanted a bride for his son Isaac, so he sent a servant into a foreign country to find a wife. Upon meeting Rebekah, the unnamed servant spoke only of his rich master and his master's handsome son. The servant providing evidence of the family's wealth by lavishing Rebekah with riches and treasures. After these extravagant attempts to glorify his master's family, the servant "proposed" to Rebekah, asking her to leave her mother and father and be joined to Isaac. Intrigued, Rebekah agreed to the servant's request and veiled herself for the journey.

As they moved toward Canaan and nearer to the wedding date,

conversations between Rebekah and the servant grew more revealing. She sought more information about her husband-to-be and inquired about him to the servant. "What is my husband like? What color is his hair? How tall is he? How gentle is his spirit? How much money does he have?" Anticipation grew, excitement heightened, and finally....

The servant and bride-to-be came upon Isaac as he was meditating in the field. The sun was setting upon the horizon and evening fell upon the land with a gentle hush. Isaac spotted the approaching caravan and began to hum the tune "Here comes the bride." Rebekah, escorted by the servant, was brought before Isaac and the two were formally introduced. Isaac smiled and found delight in his new bride. The wedding plans immediately swung into full motion.

In the same manner that Father Abraham sent a servant into the land to seek out a bride for his son, God the Father sends His servant, the Holy Spirit, into the world to search for a bride for Christ. The servant remains unnamed, for the Holy Spirit never speaks of Himself. Instead, He focuses on glorifying God and testifying about Christ. He goes to the well of the baptismal pool to find a wife for God's Son.

How miraculous is the calling of the Holy Spirit! He shares innumerable treasures and incredible gifts with the bride to confirm the goodness of the Father and the greatness of the Son. How precious are the gifts of the Holy Spirit!

He prepares the bride for her wedding, revealing more and more information about the groom during the journey. How beautiful is the teaching ministry of the Holy Spirit!

As the Bride of Christ, we continually grow in anticipation and excitement at the prospect of finally meeting our groom face to face. The sun is now setting and we observe the end-time shadows lengthening toward the culmination of history. Soon the Holy Spirit will carry us into the eternal presence of the returning Christ where we shall forever abide in His precious love.

"The sky shall unfold, preparing His entrance,

The stars shall applaud Him with thunders of praise.

The sweet light in His eyes shall enhance those awaiting,

And we shall behold Him, face to face.

The angel will sound the sound of His coming,

The sleeping shall rise from their slumbering place.

The church of Jesus Christ should be the most exciting place on earth because we are a *bridal church*. We possess an intimacy with Christ that is unique! He loves us with total, selfless devotion. He prepares us for our glorious wedding by washing our robes with the water of the Word. He destines us for a wedding ceremony glorious that the royal weddings of Buckingham Palace will pale in comparison. The church pulsates with life and love; overflowing with dreams and delight—we are a bridal church!

The Seduction of the False Bride

Satan is in the business of imitating every good thing that God creates. Satan is a copy-cat—he is not very original. The only thing he ever invented was lying and he truly owns the patent on that! Even Jesus called him the "Father of lies." In everything else, Satan simply steals God's original plan and distorts it into a cheap mimicry.

Since Christ has a bride, Satan wants a bride. Satan's bride is not the bride of Frankenstein, but the bride of the Anti-Christ. We are given a portrait of this false bride in Revelation 17. She is depicted as a drunken harlot seated on a hideous animal. She holds a filthy cup of wine in her extended hand, beckoning anyone who is willing to drink its perversion.

The bride of Satan will be a false religious system that is in alliance with the world dictator, the Anti-Christ. This religious system will consist of apostate Christianity, eastern mysticism, Middle Eastern military religions, and thousands of strange cults. All of the humanistic religious expressions of the world will unite into an impressive organization to support the rising career of the Anti-Christ.

If we were to enroll in a "False Religion Cooking Class," the recipe for baking our own religion would be quite simple. Just as there are various types of cakes, there are various types of religions. So the class would be quite diverse. Some cakes are multi-layered. Some are light. Some are rich. Some have nuts. No matter how different these cakes may be, each cake begins with the same basic ingredients; flour, salt, baking soda, butter, and eggs.

In the same way, each false religion possesses some basic ingredients common to all. Here are some of the basic ingredients that are used to start new and false religions:

➤ Claim to have divine inspiration.

➤ Make God more like humans.

➤ Make humans more like God.

➤ Write a book or start a magazine.

➤ Develop a bunch of rules and regulations.

➤ Blend ideas together from various religions.

Let the whole mixture bake (or half-bake) for a few years and—VOILA! We will have our very own religion. Satan enjoys these cooking classes, and he will be right there in the kitchen to help us along the way. Satan *loves* false religion and fallen man eats it up too. Evangelist Billy Sunday used to say, "A lie will travel around the world while truth is snapping on his boots."

Eventually, this multitude of false religions will find unity and connection under the orchestration of the False Prophet, a religious power-house who will promote the political ambitions of the Anti-Christ. This religious conglomeration will be the bride of Satan. Even today we witness the formation of this hideous bride. So many churches disguised with Christian names are moving in the direction of theological liberalism and doctrinal apostasy.

The Council of World Churches seeks unity at the expense of truth. This massive ecumenical movement seems impressive—"Let's be Unified"—but it is a unification without apostolic foundation. Their teachings amount to a horrendous hodge-podge of false doctrine seeking the lowest common denominator to achieve unity.

The old-time preacher, G. W. Lane, was waiting in his car for his wife to come out of the shopping center. While listening to the radio, Lane heard a preacher advocating for this unholy unity. "We are making good progress in our efforts of unity, but we still have obstacles. There are still some churches holding out! They are stubborn about some things. They still insist that we believe in the virgin birth of Christ. They insist that we must submit to the authority of the Bible, viewing it as the inerrant word of God. They still won't allow practicing homosexuals to be ordained. They still preach against adultery and fornication. They are slowing down the process for unity. If they would get out of the way, we could achieve these noble goals of universal unity." Extremely aggravated, Lane shouted at the radio, "Quit shoving, Mister! We're leaving anyhow!"

The Bride of Christ will be removed from earth and translated to heaven. After the rapture takes place, the "unifying" work of the False Prophet will be much easier. But even now the mystery of iniquity is at work and there is pressure placed on the true church to surrender doctrinal purity and moral piety. The bride of the Anti-Christ is seductive and appealing—she is literally dressed to kill! She will be worldly and wealthy, getting people drunk on political power. The true church of Jesus Christ must exercise discernment and discipline to resist the temptation presented by this dazzling harlot.

Let us always remember that union with Satan is always a bondage and a destruction. Revelation 17 reveals that the Anti-Christ will eventually murder his wife. Christ loves the church, but Satan does not love his wife. Satan only desires to use the church for his gain and then, after using her, he will destroy her. Joining forces with the devil is a deadly deception.

The Sanctification of the True Bride

The church I presently lead has a lovely bridal room that is used for weddings. It is in that room that the bride makes her final preparations for the wedding march. It's somewhat ironic and humorous that our lovely bridal room with large, overstuffed chairs also functions as a counseling room during the week. (Not all marriages end up in the counseling room, but many do!)

I told my church that the entire sanctuary is a bridal room. We come to church and worship to get ready for the Marriage Supper of the Lamb! If each church would see the sanctuary as a bridal room – what a difference that would make in the atmosphere! When we see ourselves as the bride of Christ, then love for Christ and love for one another become the passion and priority.

I have a minister friend who describes a wedding he officiated in which total disaster developed. One hour before the ceremony, the wedding party went outside with the photographer to find a pretty spot for some pictures. They found one, but it meant walking through a small depression made squishy by some early morning showers. Everyone stepped lightly and hiked up their pant legs and dresses. The pictures were captured successfully, but the return trip brought disaster.

The bride, walking on her tiptoes in shoes she wasn't used to, turned her ankle when she tried to sidestep a small puddle. She screamed, and her future husband grabbed her arm as she was going down... but he was not quick enough, and she splashed down in the mud. Oh the horror! The glossy white fabric of the wedding dress was stained with mud. Panic set in, and for the next hour they worked like crazy to get the mud out. There was crying, consoling, scrubbing, blaming, questioning, and more scrubbing. At wedding time, the stains were less conspicuous but still visible.

Unfortunately, that young woman is not the only mud-splattered bride I know. The church—the bride of Christ—is often smeared with handfuls of dirt by those who make it a hobby to complain, criticize, and accuse. Many from inside the church have no hesitation in slinging mud on the Bride of Christ.

One woman worked as a hairdresser. She had been quite involved in her local church but got a little upset at some decisions made by leadership. She turned her salon into a platform to bad-mouth the church. Several of her customers were attenders of the same church, and as they sat in the chair for hours of hairdos, she went on and on with negative talk about the church. What an opportunity she had with her captive audience to bless the church with her words! Instead, she picked up buckets of dirt and threw globs of it on the white robes of Christ's bride.

The church is not perfect—it is made of imperfect people! Even Christ knows that! He is constantly washing and perfecting the church with the ministry of His Word. One day, He will achieve the ultimate success, presenting to Himself a bride without spot or wrinkle. What a contrast— Satan will murder his wife, and Christ will glorify His wife. Don't be foolish enough to throw mud on the bride. Love the bride as Christ loves His bride!

A DISCIPLESHIP CHURCH

Matthew 16:21-28

From that time Jesus began to show to His disciples that He must go to Jerusalem, and suffer many things from the elders and chief

priests and scribes, and be killed, and be raised the third day. Then Peter took Him aside and began to rebuke Him, saying, "Far be it from You, Lord; this shall not happen to You!" But He turned and said to Peter, "Get behind Me, Satan! You are an offense to Me, for you are not mindful of the things of God, but the things of men." Then Jesus said to His disciples, "If anyone desires to come after Me, let him deny himself, and take up his cross, and follow Me. For whoever desires to save his life will lose it, but whoever loses his life for My sake will find it. For what profit is it to a man if he gains the whole world, and loses his own soul? Or what will a man give in exchange for his soul? For the Son of Man will come in the glory of His Father with His angels, and then He will reward each according to his works. "Assuredly, I say to you, there are some standing here who shall not taste death till they see the Son of Man coming in His kingdom."

I have a minister friend by the name of Raymond Culpepper. He is a mighty minister. In fact, some years ago he started a church in Birmingham, Alabama. They now run well over 2,000 people and they have built beautiful buildings. They are doing great work for God. Brother Culpepper shared with me a little story.

90

He had just married Peggy. They were still students at Lee University and just two weeks into their marriage. It was a Saturday, they were supposed to go to the neighborhood park for a class activity at 11 a.m.. Only, he forgot to tell Peggy about it. It was now 10:30 am, so he marched into the apartment, "Peggy, get ready. We have to go to the park for a big, big classroom function."

She said, "What?" He said, "We got to go, get ready, let's go." She said, "What?" He replied, "At 11am we have to be at the big activity." She said, "I'm not going." He said, "Yes, you are going. You know I'm studying to be a minister and I've learned about the husband being head of the house, you're going." She said, "Darling, you know this isn't fair. You didn't tell me about it. I didn't know about this. And I had other things going on. I haven't showered, my hair is a mess, and I'm not just throwing something on and going there." He said, "You are going to the park." She said, "I'm not." He said, "If I'm going, you are going." She said, "I won't do it."

He stomped out, jumped in his little car, put it in reverse, and squealed out of the parking space and went on down to the park. He got out of the car, slammed his door and acted cool for everybody. Everybody was asking, "Where is your wife? Where is your new bride? We want to see the new bride." He made excuses and felt embarrassed.

He left early with his rage building up and peaking to the point of explosion. He thought of a little sermon by which he could scorch his wife. He got home, stormed into the house, "We're are going to talk. You embarrassed me today. Everybody wanted to see the new bride. I was there and you are home being insubordinate and in rebellion. There is to be order! Peggy, you used to be so sweet. You used to be so kind. You used to be so tender. Peggy, in two weeks you've changed." She said, "No Raymond, I haven't changed. You just didn't know me."

In our relationship with Jesus Christ, sometimes we get a little bit frustrated and flustered. We say, "Jesus you used to be so sweet, but you've changed." And He says, "No, you just didn't know me."

Christianity involves the call to discipleship! The most popular nomenclature we now embrace is *Christian*. But the name *Christian* is only found three times in the New Testament. The word **disciple** is found

216 times. You are a disciple! If you are a believer, that's who you are—a disciple.

What does this really mean to be a disciple of Jesus Christ? It is all found in our text.

Discipleship involves five things:

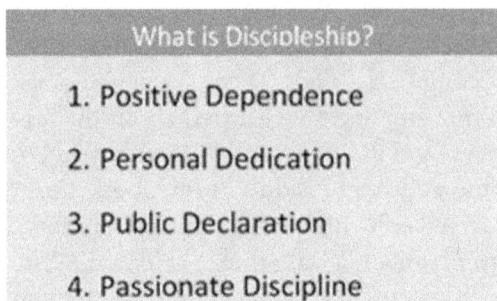

What is Discipleship?

1. Positive Dependence

2. Personal Dedication

3. Public Declaration

4. Passionate Discipline

Positive Dependence

The whole text is about the cross of the Lord Jesus Christ.

Oh, the price He paid!

The disciples at this point didn't really understand the centrality of the Cross. This was about two and half years into the public ministry of Jesus. With the crucifixion being just a year into the future, Jesus felt the need to get very blunt and plain with His disciples concerning that event. The disciples had great expectations of golden and messianic manifestation of the kingdom of God on earth with all of its pomp and glory.

We read in Mark 10 how the disciples were jockeying for position in that kingdom. "I want to be at the right hand and I want to be the left hand and I want to have a high spot in this kingdom organization." They were thinking politically. They were thinking about getting appointments that would be very prestigious. They really did not understand true definition of greatness and the path to glory. They did not understand the way of

Cross. Very directly Jesus then said, "Guys, come in close. Let me talk to you in very simple terms. I'm going to go to Jerusalem. I'm going to suffer many things. They are going to kill me. And then I'm going to be raised on the third day."

Peter was agitated for this was an astonishing announcement. Peter pulled Jesus aside to give him a little bit of a lesson in theology and a little pep talk. "Jesus, you know this will not happen; this will end the plans we all have. This isn't what I signed up for. This is not why we left our nets to follow you. You've changed." Jesus sharply said," Get behind me Satan. You do not savor the things that are of God, you're thinking like men. You are an offense to me Peter."

Interestingly, the word "offense" means "stone of stumbling." One minute prior to this, Jesus commended Peter for his affirmation of faith and said, "Upon this rock I will build my church." But now this foundation stone became a stumbling stone. When we lose our focus on the Cross of Christ, we lose our footing and we open the door for Satan to move in with his schemes.

Jesus demands the centrality of His Cross. Jesus will tell his disciples they have a cross to bear. But we need to make a distinction between the Cross of Christ and the cross we bear. The Cross of Jesus was a saving cross. On the Cross, Jesus paid it all. On the Cross, Jesus drank the bitter cup and emptied the cup of wrath until it was dry. On the Cross, Jesus satisfied a holy God and He bore the curse of transgression. He did the work of salvation on the Cross—that is what saves us. The cross we are called upon to carry is not a saving cross.

There's only one thing that saves us, and that is the Cross of the Lord Jesus Christ. That's the saving Cross. No matter how much we advance in discipleship, we have one testimony "Nothing in my hand I bring; simply to the Cross I cling."

Discipleship starts with a positive dependence. We fully trust in the Cross of the Lord Jesus Christ for acceptance with God. Our zeal for and dedication to discipleship can never be a basis for our justification.

Personal Dedication

Jesus said, "If anyone desires to come after me, **let him deny himself**" What does that mean?

Notice He didn't say "despise" yourself. That's a horrible thing to be down on yourself. A pop song says, "She doesn't bring me anything but down." Do you have people in your life who just put you down? Some people really are crippled with low self-image.

Maybe it's because of deprivation in childhood. Maybe it's because important influences in their lives injured them with negative labels. Often low esteem comes from the pain of rejection. Some who have physical features that are unattractive feel like they can't fit into a modern glamour society. Then we live in a competitive world, a "dog eat dog world," and it's easy to feel like a dog.

We live in a world of technology in which we are reduced down to a number, not even a name. Then there are philosophers who describe humans as mere machines who are manipulated with conditioned responses and that genre of anthropology just strips us of all personal dignity.

It's not God's will for a person to despise himself. Jesus came to lift humanity with a sense of self-worth and to affirm the value of every person. He had courteous conversations with women in public. He allowed children to come and sit on his lap. He allowed lepers to come and approach him. He allowed prostitutes to anoint his feet. He reached out to those segments of society that were racially discriminated against. He went through Samaria while others went the other way. He gave dignity to each human being. He was even a friend of the publicans.

I heard about a traveling circus and in this circus there was a strong man. Oh, this man was strong. He had huge hands that could grip and crunch things. He'd take a sponge that was saturated with water and would squeeze it and squeeze it until all the water was drained out, leaving the sponge dry. Then he would give a challenge, "I will give a $100 bill to any person who can come up here to squeeze another drop out of this sponge." A man came forward, he was diminutive in size and frail looking. He had small, dainty hands. He grabbed the dried out sponge and squeezed it until three drops emerged. The crowd erupted with amazement and applause. The strong man was absolutely astounded as he gave him the $100 bill. "Who are you?" To which the man replied, "I work for the IRS."

The tax collectors in the day of Christ they weren't loved. There were really despised because they were considered thieves and traitors to Israel. Jesus approached an infamous tax collector and invited him to lunch. Zacchaeus leaped out of that sycamore tree and testified to salvation. Jesus proved to be a friend of sinners. He valued people, everybody. So when Jesus said, "Deny yourself," He didn't mean belittle yourself and despise yourself.

"Deny yourself" means to reject self-idolatry, self-centeredness, and self-absorption. We are beautiful because we are made in the image of God. That divine image is to be expressed, affirmed and celebrated. That is where true dignity is demonstrated. Everything that God makes is good. But we are fallen creatures so that divine image is blurred and distorted. Everything that is ugly with sin and selfishness is to be severely rejected. A man who is all wrapped up in himself is a mighty small package.

Public Declaration

Jesus said, "If anyone who desires to come after me let him… **take up his cross.**"

Do you carry a cross out in public?

Today we buy crosses that serve as beautiful decorations. Crosses can be sparkling, sentimental pieces of jewelry that we wear around the neck or as a bracelet. Artistic crosses are tattooed onto the human body. We construct tall steeples crowned with glittering crosses and place those steeples on the roofs of our sanctuaries. These are beautiful expressions that have aesthetic appeal and warm emotional evocation.

In the first century, there was no jeweler selling or promoting crosses except Rome. The government wanted to strike fear in the hearts of people. The highways were lined with crosses upon which rebels were tortured and crucified. This was an instrument of painful capital punishment. That is what the cross was all about. You didn't talk about a cross in polite, public conversation.

Think about going to your neighbor's house. All of a sudden, your neighbor says, "Come on in and have a sandwich with me for lunch." So you go to into your neighbor's house and it's kind of weird because in the living room there's this big, life-size lethal injection bed right there in the living room. Then you go into the dining room to eat the sandwich, and you see a big portrait of an electric chair and a man being electrocuted. Then you go into the nursery to see the baby. Hanging over the crib is a little hangman's noose dangling from the mobile.

Now, what would you do? I'll tell you this, you wouldn't send your kids to that house to have a play date. Because those three things are instruments of pain and shame. We don't talk about those things or entertain images of those things. That's the way it was in the first century. That is what the cross was about—shame. So when Jesus said, "If you are going to be my disciple you must carry a cross" that was shocking.

That means that the Christian is to be willing to bear shame for the sake of Christ in front of a watching, scornful world. We don't want to feel shame. We don't want to be embarrassed, we care about what people think of us. This is the difficulty of discipleship. This world system still has a spirit that is hostile toward Christ. When believers stand up for the name of Christ and confess Him before man, that is truly bearing a cross of shame. Christians will feel that sting of persecution.

There was a man preaching downtown and he was being evangelistic. He had the sandwich board on his body. On the front were the words, "I'm a fool for Christ." People walking down the street toward him saw those words and nodded. "He is fool, look at him. What a foolish man, look at him preaching." But then they passed him, looked back and saw the words on the back of sandwich board. There was a question written, "Who's fool are you?"

We all act a little foolish at times. During the holidays, we go to office parties where executives with three piece suits have too much to drink and put lamp shades on their heads and dance on the desks. We go to football games, paint our faces and jump up and down in the freezing cold. People go to the nightclub to dance. There is nothing wrong with going dancing, but some people don't need to dance. They are like Elaine on *Seinfeld*.

Then there is karaoke. I appreciate people going to a little place to get a chance to sing. I remember one night I was at a karaoke place and I decided to sing, "You're once, twice, three times a lady." While I was singing it, I felt like I was Lionel Richie, but I wasn't. There are intelligent people who drive fancy cars, like a Lexus, BMW or Mercedes, and they get road rage. They weave in and out of traffic with red faces, obscenities coming out of their mouths, and waving to everybody with a fifth of their hands. We have seniors who determine to preserve their youthful appearances. They get liposuction, lip enhancement and surgery to stretch their eyes. Often this helps, but sometimes it just looks scary.

The point is this – it doesn't matter who we are and how cool and sophisticated we think we are, we all act foolish sometimes. We all play the fool sometimes. The question is, "Are you going to be a fool for Christ or just a fool?"

I had a church member who was so excited about his conversion. He would often rise up and testify with these words, "I'm a nut! But I'm screwed on to the right bolt."

"Therefore Jesus also, that He might sanctify the people with His own blood, suffered outside the gate. Therefore let us go forth to Him, outside the camp, bearing His reproach. For here we have no continuing city, but we seek one to come" (Hebrews 13:12-14).

Passionate Discipline

If you come after me...**follow me."**

Jesus was a peripatetic rabbi—that was His real title. A periscope is an instrument that looks around. Peripatetic is someone who walks around. Aristotle was a peripatetic philosopher. He didn't have a classroom where students gathered. He walked around. He walked through parks, rows of trees, through towns and his students followed him.

Jesus was that kind of a rabbi. He was a peripatetic teacher. He was on the move. He liked to walk and his disciples would follow. And so when Jesus said "follow me," He was saying "Join my school and learn." It was an invitation to enroll in the college of Jesus Christ and submit to His yoke of instructions.

When you join any school, there is discipline. The word "discipline" is in the word "discipleship." I serve as the president of Calvary Christian College in Waldorf, MD. I know what kind of discipline is required for success in this academic journey. You have to show up to class, listen to lectures, participate in discussions, take notes, read books, write papers, take tests and meet deadlines. There are disciplines demanded in any institution of learning.

Following Jesus as His students places upon us disciplines that will make us successful in our pursuit of Christ-likeness. There are disciplines of prayer, solitude, silence, meditation, research, corporate worship, simplicity, small things, service, submission, rejoicing, resting, fasting, and more. All these disciplines are a part of the school of Jesus.

My youngest daughter was awarded a Ph.D. program at the University of Kansas. She was given a prestigious "fellowship." Paul celebrated his fellowship with Christ, "That I might know Him in the power of His resurrection, and the fellowship of His sufferings, being conformed to His death." Our disciplines become delights as we learn of Jesus Christ and share a special intimacy with Him.

Permanent Dividends

To succeed in any school requires that the student has proper motivation. The journey can get wearisome. Especially mid-way into the semester. This is when students must keep their minds on the goal of graduation and the wonderful benefits that flow from possessing a degree. Jesus wanted to encourage His disciples to pursue this life of discipleship in spite of its difficulties. Jesus said, "If you lose yourself, you find yourself. You will discover who you truly are to be in discipleship."

This means you will find satisfaction and usefulness in this life. But Discipleship will not only shape you for an amazing life on earth, but there will be eternal rewards. "One day the Son of Man is going to come in the glory of His Father. The angels are going to come and there are going to be rewards. Each one according to his works! Some here will not taste death until you see the coming of the Son of Man" (Matthew 16:25-28 free paraphrase from author). Jesus fulfilled His promise that "some would not taste death until they had seen the coming of the Son of Man." This took place in the story that follows in Matthew 17. This is the remarkable account of the transfiguration of our Lord.

Jesus took Peter, James and John on a high mountain. Moses and Elijah showed up, the glory cloud came, the Father's voice could be heard, and Jesus was transfigured. His face was shining and his garments became white and beaming. It was an amazing experience. Here was a dress rehearsal for the Second Coming. Here was a little glimpse of eternal glory. Christ was setting forth a principle-we must always see the cross in the light of eternal glory.

On a warm summer day of 2015 I went into little haircut shop near my office to get my hair cut. They had a new computer procedure that made it a complicated registering system. With frustration I decided to take my messy hair and find a shop that would be easier to enter.

I stumbled into the mall to find a new salon which happens to be next to Macy's. I thought that if any place is next to Macy's, it's got to be good. I met Bridgette, the beautician, and she said she was available to cut my hair. While she was doing my hair, she saw all the stitches and crazy scars in my skull and she asked me about them. I was able to tell her about my 2002 crash appointment in which I was hit by an 18 wheeler truck, resulting in a long hospital stay and 60 staples drilled into my head. She was impressed that I was still alive. Then she proceeded to tell me her miracle story.

During the holiday season of 2010, her husband was only in his 40's and on his death bed. He needed two lungs but he had an unusual blood type, and it was hard to get a donor. On December 24th; Christmas Eve, they received a phone call from John Hopkins, "Come to the hospital, we have two lungs that are available." So they rushed to the hospital. It was a successful double lung transplant.

For over five years they had been searching for the donor because they wanted to know who passed and who gave these lungs, however all the information was blocked. In April, 2015, a lady who had never been to Waldorf entered the St. Charles Towne Center Mall and randomly walked into this same salon where Bridgette works.

They struck up a conversation and the woman talked about how her husband passed away on December 23, five years ago. For some reason Bridgette asked, "Was he a donor?" The woman replied "Yes, In fact he was a donor. He died on December 23, and I gave strict instructions that all his body parts were to be received on December 24 as a Christmas gift before Christmas Day." Bridgette asked, "In what hospital did he die?" Then the answer came, "Johns Hopkins."

Out of that conversation, they researched, made phone calls and found out that he was the donor. Bridgette and this stranger to Waldorf became dear friends. They now walk together in the annual Baltimore parade called the Walk of the Living Legacy. Bridgette and her husband were so thankful to know the donor.

I want to know my Donor. I want to know who made my spiritual life possible. You see, I was dying, my lungs were failing and God gave me heavenly breath. He gave me two new lungs and He gave me spiritual life. Jesus went to the Cross and gave Himself that I might live. That I might have life more abundantly. I want to know my donor. And that is why I'm a disciple of Christ.

AN IMPERFECT CHURCH

Romans 7:15-25

For what I am doing, I do not understand. For what I will to do, that I do not practice; but what I hate, that I do. If, then, I do what I will not to do, I agree with the law that it is good. But now, it is no longer I who do it, but sin that dwells in me. For I know that in me (that is, in my flesh) nothing good dwells; for to will is present with me, but how to perform what is good I do not find. For the good that I will to do, I do not do; but the evil I will not to do, that I practice. Now if I do what I will not to do, it is no longer I who do it, but sin that dwells in me. I find then a law, that evil is present with me, the one who wills to do good. For I delight in the law of God according to the inward man. But I see another law in my members, warring against the law of my mind, and bringing me into captivity to the law of sin which is in my members. O wretched man that I am! Who will deliver me from this body of death? I thank God—through Jesus Christ our Lord! So then, with the mind I myself serve the law of God, but with the

flesh the law of sin.

A man and his wife were driving their RV across the country. They were nearing the big city in Kentucky called Louisville. They noted the strange spelling and tried to figure out how to pronounce it. "Is it Louis – ville? Is it Luu - vulle? Is it Loey - ville?" They grew more perplexed as they drove into town.

Since they were hungry, they pulled into a restaurant to get something to eat. At the counter, the man said to the cashier, "My wife and I can't seem to be able to figure out how to pronounce this place. Will you tell me where we are and say it very slowly so I can understand?" The waitress looked at him and said, "Buuuuurrrgerrr Kiiiinnng."

There are many words which are difficult to pronounce perfectly. In fact, there are *many* things at which we are imperfect. When it comes to the Christian life, we are not perfect in practicing it. This turns some people off concerning the church. "Oh, I don't bother going to church—it's filled with hypocrites." It is true that there are hypocrites in *every* church; people who, like a snake, shed their skin but still keep the sting.

Every local assembly is plagued with its pretenders and play actors. Most church folk are not hypocrites, just imperfect. Being imperfect does not make us hypocrites. Authentic Christians possess a reality of faith, but learning to fully express that faith and put it in shoe leather is not easy.

I know some people who are always hopping from one church to another, looking for that perfect church. Listen! If you find the perfect church, don't join it—if you join it, you will ruin it! You are not perfect. No church is perfect. Christians are not perfect because we struggle with a sinful nature. Let's divide this message of an imperfect church into two parts: the conflict of the struggle and the comfort in the struggle.

The Conflict Described

The language of the opening text of this section (Romans 7:15-25) is extremely depressing. It is filled with defeatism, giving rise to much debate as to whom Paul is actually talking about. Does he speak of the unsaved man? Or perhaps an immature Christian who has not yet grown in the Lord? Or maybe even an unsanctified Christian who has yet to tap into the power of the Holy Spirit? Let's explore some of these various interpretations.

Some say Paul is referring to the unsaved man. They argue that when he uses the present tense to describe his conflict with sin, he is really just employing a literary technique to refer to his pre-conversion days. It is apparent to me, however, that this passage cannot be referring to the unregenerate. The person in this picture is a saved person.

Paul speaks of his inner man as having strong desires to please God and obey His law. The righteousness of the inner man can only come into existence through the miracle of new spiritual birth.

In the poem *Maud*, Alfred Tennyson depicts the yearning of a certain character, "Ah, for a new man to rise in me, that the man I am may cease to be." The Christian can say that a new man has arisen in him, one with newfound spiritual appetites and affections.

In verse 22, Paul says that the inward man delights in the law of God, a description that can only be applied to a saved believer. An unbeliever cannot delight in the law of God. In fact, Romans 8:7 says that the unsaved man has an inner hostility towards God.

Another indication that Paul is speaking of the saved man is that he truly laments about sin clinging to him, describing his condition with anguish and grief. Before Paul was converted, he did not grieve over sin. He couldn't even see his sinfulness! He was smug in self-righteousness. Philippians 3:6 tells us that he was self-satisfied, thinking himself blameless before God's law. Only the born again believer has the capacity to truly love God's righteousness and abhor sinfulness.

A flippant teenager said to a preacher, "You talk about a weight of sin, but I feel nothing. How heavy is sin? Ten pounds? Eighty pounds? One hundred pounds?"

The pastor gently responded, "Let me ask you something. If you laid a four-hundred pound weight upon a corpse, would it feel the load?"

The teen answered, "No, it would feel nothing because it is dead."

The pastor pressed home his point: "So it is with the soul that is spiritually dead. It too is incapable of sensing the heavy load of sin. Such a person is indifferent to the burden of sin and uncaring about its presence."

Ephesians 2:1-3 tells us that sinners are dead in sins and trespasses. They are not worried about their sinful state because they are lifeless in the grave yard of iniquity. On the contrary, those who have life in Christ are hypersensitive to the presence of sin. Therefore, we can safely conclude that Paul does not describe an unsaved man in this passage.

Another theory concludes that Paul must be describing an immature Christian who has not yet learned to walk in victory. The belief is that a Christian can "grow out" of Romans Chapter 7 as he grows in the Lord. However, when Paul wrote this passage, he *was* a mature, seasoned apostle.

It is the mature Christian who has developed an acute sensitivity toward the heights of God's law and the depths of personal depravity. God is light, and the closer we get to God, the more that light will expose faults and failures that plague us. The spiritually mature possess profound insight into God's perfection and human imperfection: producing personal brokenness, contrition, and humility.

This is not the only place where Paul laments about his sinful condition. In Ephesians 3:8 he speaks of himself as the very least of all the saints. In I Timothy 1:12-15 he speaks of himself as the chief of sinners. As a believer grows in his spiritual life, he inevitably will have an increased hatred of sin and an increased love for truth and holiness. As these desires increase, the sense of struggle will intensify. This passage is the language and lament of a spiritually mature Christian.

Some interpret this passage as describing a Christian who has not yet experienced the blessing of sanctification. "Oh, how pathetic—this person has not tapped into the deeper spiritual life. This person is too carnal. He has not yet been sanctified." Beloved, there are not two categories of Christians—those sanctified and those not sanctified. All Christians are sanctified. Paul wrote to the Christians of Corinth, addressing them as sanctified ones, even though they had all kind of carnal issues (I Corinthians 1:2).

There is no transformational experience at a revival service or special prayer conference that can remove a believer from the sinful struggle. There is no one-time powerful encounter with God that will change the Christian's humanness into spiritual molecules. Some churches teach that the Christian can come to the place of sinless perfection while walking the earth. But Paul says the contrary. In Philippians 3:12 Paul admits that he falls short of perfection. However, instead of allowing this to defeat him, he determined to forget the things of the past and reach forward to the high calling of God.

As Christians, we have not yet reached our destination. We are travelers, not settlers. We are pilgrims on the journey. As long as we are on this side of the grave, we will struggle with temptation, failure, frustration, and discouragement.

Romans 7 describes the struggle of *every* Christian. There is sin within. Christ dwells within the heart of the believer, but sin dwells in the flesh of the believer. The Christian loathes this tension of mixed desires. He longs to be rid of the sin that stubbornly clings to his flesh.

The Comfort Declared

Let us not grow discouraged in the conflict! In the midst of this deep inward struggle, the Christian possesses joy and confidence. We must examine Romans 7 in its context as it is arranged in the Book of Romans.. Notice it is sandwiched between Romans 6 and Romans 8. We cannot isolate our text and make it the total sum of the Christian life. What comfort does God provide so that this sinful struggle does not drive us to despair?

The Position of Power

"For sin shall not have dominion over you, for you are not under law but under grace." — Romans 6:14

In Romans 6, Paul builds the teaching that, for the believer, the authority, control, and captivity of sin have been broken. This emancipation puts us in a position opposite of sin so that we can declare war against it. The Christian fights with the forces of sin and sometimes is defeated, but this very warfare stands as proof that sin is no longer a master we serve, but an enemy we fight. This is great news!

What a change! At one time, sin was our master; we had to obey that master and bow to its rule. Thanks to Jesus, we are no longer servants of sin. Sin is no longer our master, and we are not obligated to obey its commands. Sin is now the enemy, and we can resist it and wrestle against it. We have been set free from servitude. Think about how exciting this truth is for us!

The continuous struggle with sin reminds us that we belong to a new allegiance—no longer friends with the devil, but sworn enemies. We are not floating downstream with the world. Instead, we are swimming upstream. Yes, we swim constantly against the current, but at least we swim *in the right direction*. As my mother always says, "If the devil is not fighting you, then he already has you." Christians find comfort because we have a position of power.

Proclamation of Pardon

"There is therefore now no condemnation to those who are in Christ Jesus." — Romans 8:1

The believer is free from all condemnation. This is not something we are hoping will happen in the distant future. We are not in suspense about our status— "Will I go to heaven or will I go to hell?" We are not on the edge of our seats wondering what the verdict will be. The verdict is in; the judgment is made. The Judge has already passed His decision— "There is now *no* condemnation to those who are in Christ Jesus" (Romans 8:1)

What encouragement to us as we grapple with sinfulness! During our struggle with sin, we often feel condemnation. Yet the Bible declares us not condemned. Instead of the burden of condemnation, we are convicted of the Spirit and corrected by the Heavenly Father. When we yield to the flesh, we grieve the precious Spirit of God. When the Spirit is miserable, we will be miserable. This, however, is not condemnation; it is training so that we can live in continual repentance and renewal.

Daily contrition and confession connect us to the fellowship of God in a deep and profound way. The Prophet Isaiah said, "For all those things My hand has made, and all those things exist says the Lord, but on this one will I look: on him who is poor and of a contrite spirit. And who trembles at My word" (Isaiah 66:1-2) We have comfort because of the proclamation of pardon.

Presence of Pentecost

"For what the law could not do in that it was weak through the flesh, God did by sending His own Son in the likeness of sinful flesh, on account of sin: He condemned sin in the flesh, that the righteous requirement of the law might be fulfilled in us who do not walk according to the flesh but according to the Spirit." — *Romans 8:3-4*

Did you notice something conspicuously absent from our text in Romans 7? In the description of the conflict, there is no mention of the Holy Spirit. The battle is between the inner man of the Christian and the flesh of the Christian. Moving into Chapter 8, however, we read about the Holy Spirit who resides within the Christian, supplying every believer with an ally for battle. The Holy Spirit gives strength to the inner man so that the flesh is outnumbered and overpowered. This is the key to victory—depending on the Holy Spirit and walking in the energy and strength that the Spirit provides.

The day of Pentecost brought forth the dispensational fullness of the Holy Spirit so that today every believer enjoys the gift of the Spirit. Romans 8:9 says that "if anyone does not have the Spirit of Christ, he does not belong to Christ." Every Christian is Pentecostal – indwelt by the Spirit. It is by this power alone that we are enabled to experience incredible victory.

When the flesh is weak, and the devil is strong, temptation is overwhelming and the world is alluring, the Holy Spirit is our constant companion. He gives us the strength to declare, "Greater is He that is in me than he that is in the world" (I John 4:4). If we walk in the Spirit, we will not fulfill the lusts of the flesh. We have comfort because we have the presence of Pentecost.

Promise of Preservation

"Who shall separate us from the love of Christ? Shall tribulation, or distress, or persecution, or famine, or nakedness, or peril, or sword?" — Romans 8:35

Romans 8:35 raises the question, "What shall separate us from the love of Christ?" We are haunted by that question as we go through seasons of deep struggle. "When will God give up on me? Will today's failure be the one that breaks the camel's back? Will God turn His back on me? At what point will God reject me and disqualify me from His family?" If God's redemptive love is conditional, then our struggle becomes a tormenting nightmare. We would become paralyzed with fear of rejection. Fear and guilt cannot provide the right motivation for holy living. So, back to the question: "What shall separate us from the love of God?"

Paul's answer supplies believers with the promise of preservation: *"For I am persuaded that neither death nor life, nor angels nor principalities nor powers, nor things present nor things to come, nor height nor depth, nor any other created thing, shall be able to separate us from the love of God which is in Christ Jesus our Lord"* (Romans 8:38-39).

Prospect of Perfection

"O wretched man that I am! Who will deliver me from this body of death? I thank God—through Jesus Christ our Lord!" — Romans 7:24-25

Near Tarsus, where Paul was born, an ancient tribe sentenced murderers to an especially gruesome execution. The corpse of the slain person was lashed tightly to the body of the murderer and remained there until the murderer himself died. The convicted man would have this dead body on his back, and the decay of the rotting body would infect him until he died. Sometimes, the convicted man would be driven to insanity and suicide, bearing the visible shame of his crime as he carried a dead body on his back.

Perhaps this was the image Paul had in mind when he wrote the words in Romans 7:24, "O wretched man that I am, who shall deliver me from this body of death?" I'm glad that in the next breath he provides the answer, "I thank God, through our Lord Jesus Christ."

One day there will be a complete deliverance from this sinful struggle. This body of death will be lifted from us. Romans 8:18 tells us that the future glory revealed in us will far outweigh the sufferings of the present time. Romans 8:23 tells us that we are eagerly waiting for the redemption of the body. Today, the church is not perfect, but one day it will be.

A legendary Christian was on his death bed. This man had served Christ faithfully for over 60 years. He worked as a missionary, accomplishing so much for the kingdom of God. He was known for his integrity and piety. As they gathered around his death bed, his friends asked, "What is the greatest thing you can tell us? What is the greatest thing you have learned as a champion of faith?"

With a frail and weakened voice, he said, "I have learned two things: I am a great sinner, and Jesus is a great Savior."

A GREAT COMMANDMENT CHURCH

> **Matthew 22:35**
>
> Then one of them a lawyer asked Jesus a question testing him and saying, "Teacher which is the great commandment in the law? Jesus said to him, "you shall love the Lord your God with all your heart and with all your soul with all your mind. This is the first and great commandment. And the second is like it. You shall love your neighbor as yourself. On these two commandments all the law and the prophets."

A certain boy was eight years old. He was chubby and clumsy and nerdy. The big bullies were chasing him to beat up on him as they called him "Fat Freddie." As they chased him, Freddie made his way into a familiar little neighborhood. He saw a house up ahead and he knew an elderly lady who lived there. He prayed as he was running, huffing and puffing, "Oh Lord, have my neighbor see me, open the door and give me some refuge." And she did! That prayer was answered. That was part of his appreciation for the concept of neighbors and a good neighborhood. Little Freddie became that great person that we know as Mr. Rogers, or Fred Rogers.

He had an amazing life! Mr. Rogers was an ordained Presbyterian Minister out of Pittsburg. He got up every day at 5:30 a.m. to read the Bible, pray and sing hymns. He wrote over 200 songs. Every morning he would swim, and that would be his physical exercise. He was very careful about his weight. Do you know that every day of his entire adult life, he weighed 143 pounds?

That was his favorite number because he said "it takes one letter to say *I*, it takes four letters to say *love*, and it takes three letters *you*." I know that sounds a little corny. But for him, 143 symbolized "I love you." In 1992 he was receiving an honorary doctorate degree at Boston University—his 25th doctoral degree. When he was introduced, 5,000 people shot up to their feet to applaud him and cheer him. It was almost embarrassing to him such an extravagant response. He couldn't get anybody to settle down. So finally Mr. Rogers said, "Ok, everybody sit down and sing with me, "It's beautiful day in the neighborhood, the neighborhood, the neighborhood. It's a beautiful day for a neighbor. Would you be mine, would you be my neighbor?"

A mayor of a great city in California was asked, "If you could make one change to really improve this city, what would it be? If you could wave a wand and create one change that would definitely enhance this city, what would it be?" The mayor cleared his throat, stood tall and said, "Well, it's kind of embarrassingly simple, but I would train people to be better neighbors."

The biggest single factor that helps a city to flourish is for it to have a sufficient number of good neighbors. When neighbors care, then the elderly are taken care of and at-risk youth are less at risk. When neighbors care, crime goes down, volunteerism goes up, isolated people become less lonely, people get motivated about the condition of their property and the property value goes up. All of these benefits are realized when we seek to be better neighbors.

A student of the law asked Jesus, "What is the great commandment in the Law?" Of course, Jesus quoted from Deuteronomy 6:4, "Hear, O Israel: The Lord our God, the Lord *is* one! You shall love the Lord your God with all your heart, with all your soul, and with all your strength." This was the first Bible verse the Jewish people would memorize at home. This was a prayer prayed every day. It was called the **Shema** because it means "hear." And that is the way the text starts, "Hear O Israel."

Do we hear? A man went to his pastor and said, "Pastor, I need prayer." The pastor said, "Tom, what is prayer request?" To which the man said, "I need prayer for my hearing." So the pastor laid hands on him and prayed that God would open those ear drums. After the prayer the pastor asked, "Tom, do you think God answered your prayer?" The man replied, "Oh I don't know. The hearing isn't until Tuesday."

We need to hear. "Hear O Israel, the Lord God, the Lord God is one." There's one God. Monotheism was a new concept for much of the world. This was radical! "Hear, O Israel, Lord God is one. And you shall love the Lord your God."

This was also radical, that we could love this one and only God. Not just fear Him with a reverential trust, but have positive feelings for God. What a command, to have affection, passion, and delight with regard to God. The command is strong, love God and don't hold anything back. "Love the Lord your God with all your heart, your soul, your mind."

Jesus shocked those who were listening to Him that day as He quoted from Deuteronomy 6:4, because he added to the Shema a command that would have equal importance. They thought, "You can't change the Shema." That would be like us quoting the Pledge of Allegiance, but adding some words to it because we feel like it. You can't do that!

Jesus said, "This is the great commandment - love God. And the second is like unto it. – love your neighbor." The student might have protested, "Wait, I didn't ask for two. What do you mean two?" But you see, the second comes out the first. You can't have one without the other. Jesus said that the first command is to love God and the second command is to love the neighbor. He tied them both together as an inseparable unit.

You cannot succeed at life and fail at love. And you cannot fail at life if you succeed at love. Love is the most important thing. But love isn't just sentimentalism, it involves feelings. I like feelings of love. But there is nothing soft about love. Love means you have a good intention towards somebody. You wish good for somebody as God defines that good.

Loving your neighbor means you don't do certain bad things and it means we do certain good things. The Apostle Paul in Roman 12 says that if you love your neighbor, you're going to fulfill the righteousness of the Law. How that does work out? If you love your neighbor, you will not steal from him. If you love your neighbor, you will not deceive him.

If you love your neighbor, you will not murder him. If you love your neighbor, you will not mess with his wife. If you love your neighbor, you will not covet his possessions. The power of love provides the power and the proper motivation to do righteous things. This is why Jesus said that all of the Law and the Prophets hang on these two commandments.

But love isn't just restraining from doing bad things that would be injurious to your neighbor. Love puts you in a positive mode of action of good will toward your neighbor. It becomes very practical and personal. Jesus did not say, "Love a cause. Love some nameless, faceless people who live half way around the globe and are marginalized and you never have contact with them." Of course, we are supposed to treat people well who are geographically far from us. But this commandment brings us closer to home. "Love your neighbor."

The word "neighbor" comes from the word **neigh**, which means **close by**. The rest of the word, "**bor**" is Dutch for **dwelling place**. And so neighbor means "someone who dwells close by on your street, around the corner." We are to love that person. A real flesh and blood, breathing human being with whom we have contact. This takes loving out of the abstract and puts it in the concrete. It takes loving out of the general and puts it in the specific.

Our neighborhoods are different today than they were in the day of Christ. For one thing, in the day of Christ they didn't have automatic garage door openers. I know some of you drive in a big car with tinted windows. Then you press that little button on your visor and the garage door opens. You drive into that little building, and it's like your own little mote. The garage door closes behind you and you go through the kitchen. You don't even have to walk through the front yard and see anyone. In the time of Christ, neighborhoods were quite intimate. they had small, plain houses with no garages. They didn't have electricity for air-conditioning so that most people were outside more than inside. Neighborhoods were very important.

It was only 60 years ago when architects who designed homes had this really neat idea. It was called a front porch. How many of you remember a front porch? After World War II, architects got rid of the front porches and created more backyard space. Backyards with high privacy fences and hedges.

Part of "loving your neighbor" is coming out of hiding and getting to know your neighbor. If I ask you to tell me the names of your neighbors, could you answer? I'm talking about the house to your left. Do you know those folks? The house to your right and across the street - do you know your neighbors?

How did Mr. Rogers begin his daily show? He would change his shoes, put on his sneakers and tie them up. Do you know why he would lace up his shoes? He was making a point that we all need to slow down. I know of a high power businessman who would never buy sneakers or any shoes with shoe strings because he was too much in a hurry. Everything had to be loafers or slip-ons. He died at 52. The lesson - Buy shoe strings shoes!

We are rushing in and out of the house, and that's not "loving your neighbor." Get to know your neighbor. Do this by asking simple questions. Talk about their children, hobbies, vacations and gardens.

A huge part of loving a persons is slowing down and getting to know them on a personal level.

Sometimes, love is respecting the privacy of the neighbor. "He who blesses his friend with a loud voice, rising early in the morning. It will be counted a curse to him" (Proverbs 27:14). Some people want a little more space. Respect them. That's alright—you don't want to be pushy.

Some people are stand offish because there are painful things going on and they don't want exposure. Only God knows what is going on behind closed doors. You can't push the door open, but pray and love. And maybe that person will open the door to you, paving the way for a healing to take place.

The first time we see the words "love your neighbor" in the Bible, it is found in the Book of Leviticus. "Don't seek revenge to your neighbor, don't hold a grudge. Love your neighbor as yourself" (Leviticus 19:17-18).

How can I love my neighbor? Don't stay angry! Practice patience and forgiveness. Get over it! This is very relevant, because neighbors can get cranky and intrusive. Sometimes they play their music too loud.

Sometimes they shine their flood lights too brightly. Sometimes they park their three cars in your space. Sometimes their children will throw balls into your yard. Being a neighbor is not easy. But here is an opportunity to show forth the wonderful love of God.

Here is another positive expression of love, "Do not say to your neighbor, 'Go, and come back. And tomorrow I will give it. When you have it with you" (Proverbs 3:28). If your neighbor wants to borrow something and you have it, don't say "tomorrow." If you possess something that will benefit your neighbor, then share it. "But they might not return that hammer." God will always prosper generosity. Share your tools, pies, lawn chairs and space.

If there is an elderly person in your neighborhood, reach out and be kind. I wonder how many in your neighborhood are elderly? Oh, they would love to share a cup of tea with you in the afternoon. They would love to just sit and talk about their kids and grandkids and tell their war stories.

God is all about building good neighborhoods. That's exactly what He is doing in heaven. He's building a great neighborhood. Jesus said, "Let not your heart be troubled. You believe in God; believe also in Me. In My Father's house are many mansions, if it were not so, I would have told you" (John 14:1-3).

There is a debate about that word "mansion" because it can also be translated to mean "rooms." If it means *rooms*, then so be it. I'm persuaded He is not building cabins in the corner of glory. There's no debate about what kind of houses or rooms He's building in heaven. They are all mansions. It will be a fantastic neighborhood. He is preparing that place for me and preparing me for that place. And when I get there, the Lord is not going to say, "Oh there goes the neighborhood. Here's trouble, lets lock the doors. Property value is going down now." When I show up to the neighborhood and I move into my mansion, He's going to say, "Hi neighbor. Won't you be my neighbor?"

A GREAT COMMISSION CHURCH

I read an article that talked about a custom in Congress that was finally abandoned. I thought it was kind of sad. You see, for over 50 years, the House of Representatives had this neat little tradition. At the beginning of the session, they would read the Farewell Address of George Washington. It was after he had served eight years as president, and he gave a stirring speech to Congress where he challenged America to stay on target and remember the essentials.

For the first few years they read the speech, it was well attended. People were excited about it. But as time went on, interest dwindled and the attendance was less and less and less. Until finally only 10 people were showing up. So they took a vote and they voted to abandon the tradition. No more reading of the Farewell Address of George Washington.

I hope that the Christian church never abandons the farewell address of the Lord Jesus Christ. At the time, Christ had risen from the dead. He was about ready to ascend back into heaven. He gathered 500 around him and offered a speech, and he gave the church marching orders. He said, "This is our mission statement: Go into all the world and preach

117

this gospel message to every creature. Have people seal the deal by baptizing them. And use the Trinitarian Formula Father, Son, Holy Spirit. Keep in mind that the main purpose is not to make decisions, to make disciples" (Matthew 28:19; paraphrased by author).

Each church is to have a teaching ministry that is evangelistic in nature. An evangelistic appeal that is both local and global.

Every Christian should have a zeal for this mission of outreach. Like a fire without a glow, like a winter without a snow, like a river without a flow, like a conviction without a "no", like a wind without a blow, like a oar without a row, like a picture without a throw, like a harvest without a sow, like a Santa without ho, like a foot without a toe, like a gardener without a hoe, like a rooster without a crow, like a high without a low, like a buck without a doe, like an actor without a show, like a violin without a bow—it's like the Christian who will not go.

Christ said "Go." Penetrate every culture, every nation, because we have something to share. Go. Sometimes missions can be intrusive if we are imposing our culture on somebody else. But that's not missions. Missions means that we respect people's cultures and backgrounds and customs, but we enter in to share the good news that Christ is the Savior of the world.

I hope the great commission doesn't become the great omission and we forget the mission of the church. Oh, that we would be evangelistic, sharing in a tender way and a respectful way, the good news of Jesus Christ.

If we are going to fulfill the great commission, we have to do several things.

1. We have to have compassion.

2. We have to have confidence.

3. We have to have connection.

4. We have to have commitment.

We Have to Have Compassion

"Knowing therefore the terror of the Lord, we persuade men; but we are made manifest unto God." — 2 Corinthians 5:11

When Paul speaks here, we understand the seriousness of the situation. Only one third of the earth's population is of the Christian faith and that is if we count everyone who claims to be a Christian. As we know, some are nominal Christians - in name only. But if we count every person who takes the label Christian, only one third of earth's population is Christian faith. That means 4.5 billion people in our world do not embrace Jesus Christ as the Savior.

What about these other people? Are we supposed to be sharing with them? What authority do we have to do that? Christ said all authority is given to Him. Based on that authority, we can go forth with courage to touch these precious people—yes, the 4.5 billion people outside of the faith of the Lord Jesus Christ.

Now, that might not move us because it is such a big number. We get lost in statistics. It was Joseph Stalin who said the death of one is a tragedy, the death of a million is a statistic. Those are chilling words from a mad man. But there is some truth to it. Statistics can overwhelm us, but then when there is a death of one person we feel the pain of that as

119

we see ourselves reflected in that death.

It's not just 4.5 billion people in our world—these are made of individuals. Each person created in the image of God! Each person with desires and dreams and needs and wants! Each person is somebody's son, each person is somebody's daughter, each person has fear and loneliness and struggles. And for any person to be disconnected from God forever would be tragic for them as it's tragic for us. Do we have enough compassion to make a difference in our world?

We Have to Have Confidence

"For I am not ashamed of the gospel of Christ, for it is the power of God to salvation for everyone who believes..." — Romans 1:16

When I leave the hospital at Washington Hospital Center, I have to go down on Michigan and then on New York Avenue to get back onto 295. Then the traffic gets all gunked up on New York Avenue. And so I sit there at the red light, but I like sitting at that red light and I'll tell you why. Because there is the gorgeous Roman Catholic Church right on the corner and it has this big plaque on the front of the outside sanctuary that says, "Please come in, we have a story to tell."

In the Christian faith, we have a story to tell. And we should not be ashamed of our story. Now, when you communicate with people to reach people for God, you can use your story. Because God has done something for you. And people will be able to relate to your testimony.

But keep in mind, as we share our faith, that people are not saved by your life. They are saved by His death. And they need to hear how Jesus went to the cross and paid the price for our sin debt. You may find that to be a difficult assignment to share the gospel. But you don't have to be a scholar in biblical languages to qualify as a personal evangelist. If you can quote John 3:16 – that is enough gospel to save millions

"For God so loved the world that He gave His only begotten Son, that whoever believes in Him should not perish but have everlasting life." – John 3:16

The gospel of Christ is the power of God. Do you know that there is no other thing in the Bible that directly says this – "This is the power of God." And think about power. The sun's surface is 9,900 degrees Fahrenheit, and its core is 27 million degrees Fahrenheit. The tsunami in Japan had 100-feet high the waves, and it moved 80 miles per hour, destroying everything in its path. Power!

I read an article of scientists discovering a star that was streaking through our galaxy at 1.5 miles per hour. We read about a volcanoes; the lava spews miles up in the air and the sound of the explosion can be heard thousands of miles away. That's power. The power of God's creation. But none of these things are said to *be* the power of God. None of these things! There is one thing that directly says "this is the power of God" and that is gospel message

"For I am not ashamed of the Gospel of Jesus Christ for it is the power of God unto salvation…" (Romans 1:16).

Oh, we should have confidence in our marching orders. We should have confidence as we build relationships and we reach out to people in love. Because the gospel is powerful to save. The message is the method. We have to have confidence.

We Have to Have Connection

"But you shall receive power when the Holy Spirit has come upon you; and you shall be witnesses to Me in Jerusalem, and in all Judea and Samaria, and to the end of the earth..." — Acts 1:8

We can't do this on your own. We can't fulfill the great commission just through our machinery and programs and committees and getting together. We must have supernatural power to do the work of God.

Jesus really upset the disciples and they probably thought Jesus wasn't being accurate. Jesus never exaggerated or told a false hood. But when Jesus announced in the upper room "It's for your benefit that I am leaving." They probably didn't understand that.

Can you image how awesome it would be to have Jesus with you in body? Think about it! Think about if Jesus went home with you today in body and He was your buddy. Flesh and blood Jesus. Think about how awesome that would be. You would have a theological question, bam! You ask Jesus because He knows. "Jesus what does this mean?" He tells you. You're throwing a little church picnic and you've got donuts but too many people showed up and you're out of donuts but you don't worry about it, because Jesus came. You say, "Jesus we are out of donuts," and so He takes a few crumbs multiplies them and everybody gets a donut and there is a dozen leftover. Your dog gets run over. You say, "Jesus my dog! And He raises the dog from the dead.

But Jesus left. He said to his disciples, "It's to your advantage that I'm leaving, because when I leave, I'm going to the Father. I'm going to ask the Father to give you the Holy Spirit and the Holy Spirit inside of you is better than Jesus beside you" (John 16:7 author paraphrase).

Why is that? Because Jesus was confined to a human body. He was limited, in time and space. But know the Holy Spirit is in you. The Holy Spirit is in me. When we do the dismissal, nobody has to fight to see who gets to invite Jesus to dinner. The Holy Ghost goes home with all of us.

Through the indwelling presence of the Spirit we can duplicate the ministry of Jesus Christ to enlarge Christianity beyond the confines of Palestine. The gifts of the Spirit empower the church so we can witness for Him and continue what He has started on earth.

We Have to Have Commitment

"And Jesus went throughout all the cities and villages, teaching in their synagogues and proclaiming the gospel of the kingdom and healing every disease and every affliction. When he saw the crowds, he had compassion for them, because they were harassed and helpless, like sheep without a shepherd. Then he said to his disciples, 'The harvest is plentiful, but the laborers are few; therefore pray earnestly to the Lord of the harvest to send out laborers into his harvest.'"—Matthew 9:35-38

In Acts 18, we read that Paul is in jail, though not for doing wrong things but for doing right. He brought deliverance to a girl who was demon possessed and exploited by people who wanted to use her to make money. Paul, through Christ, brought deliverance to this tormented soul. And of course, it hurt the finances of the community. So Paul is beaten in Roman style and put into the inner dungeon. At midnight he's not complaining. Rather, He's singing and praising and praying.

Apparently God liked Paul's song. God got to listening to the song. The Bible says that heaven is God's throne and the earth is God's footstool. So God starts tapping his foot. "Oh, that is good singing." And tapping His foot, God cause an earthquake. This was the Jailhouse Rock. All the walls rattle, the prison doors open, chains are shattered and they are free. This was God giving Paul his freedom.

Now if I was in jail and the door was open, I'm getting out of there. I don't want to be in jail. So Paul is making his way out of the prison and the jailer is standing there with a sword against his own neck to commit suicide. The jailer knows that if he loses any prisoner, he would have to pay with his own life. Paul looks back in the shadows and see this jailer ready to take his own life. Paul is free and could have left! But he had compassion. He stops. Paul walks up to him. The jailer says, "What must I do to be saved?" Paul says, "Believe on the Lord Jesus Christ and you will be saved and your house." And the man was converted to Christ.

Sometimes we are so anxious to walk through those doors of freedom and prosper and be blessed and have a good time. And nothing is wrong with that. But is there a commitment to the work of God?

I know of a young man who finished college and was offered a job at $300,000 a year. He gave it up because he felt that he needed to get into church planting. I know a family who gave up the American dream and moved to the Middle East because they wanted to make a difference for Christ in some of those countries. I know some who live on less then they make so they can free up money to help people who are hurting and people who are lost.

I don't know what kind of assignment God has for you. God might want you just to prosper, and out of that platform of success show the glory of God and help others to succeed and lead them to the Lord. But whatever your calling, winning souls for Christ must be a passion.

You say, "This is too radical." Well, now you are getting it. Christ didn't come to make few little alterations to our lives. This is a radical thing where we are committed farewell address of the Lord Jesus.

A PRAYERFUL CHURCH

Matthew 6:9-13

Our Father in heaven,
Hallowed be Your name.
Your kingdom come.
Your will be done
On earth as *it is* in heaven.
Give us this day our daily bread.
And forgive us our debts,
As we forgive our debtors.
And do not lead us into temptation,
But deliver us from the evil one.
For Yours is the kingdom and the power and the glory
forever. Amen.

Mr. Purdue of the famed Purdue Chicken went to the pastor of a mega church and said, "Listen, we're going to give you $1 million during Sunday worship if you change the words of the Lord's Prayer. Instead of 'Give us this day our daily bread', say, 'Give us this day our daily chicken.'"

The pastor exclaimed, "We can't do that. It's impossible to change the Lord's Prayer! It's permanent!"

Mr. Purdue said, "Well, we respect your conviction… how about $10 million to change it?"

Later that week, the pastor met with the church leadership: "I have good news and bad news," he told them. "The good news is we came into $10 million dollars! The bad news is we lost the Wonder Bread account."

We all love the Lord's Prayer. In all honesty, we can't really call it "The Lord's Prayer," because our Lord never actually prayed it! It was not His personal prayer. How inappropriate for Jesus to pray, "Forgive us our trespasses." Jesus was sinless! When we refer to it as the Lord's Prayer, we are referring to the fact that it was a model prayer shared with the disciples by Jesus. We love the Lord's Prayer.

Jesus gave this prayer in response to the inquiry of the disciples. Are you surprised that they were wanting to gain insight into the life of prayer? "Lord, teach us to pray," they asked. They could have asked a lot of questions and submitted many requests. *"Jesus, Teach us to turn water into wine. Teach us to walk on water. Teach us to raise the dead."* Instead, they made the connection between the prayer life of Jesus and the powerful ministry of Jesus. They observed His solid commitment to prayer, His passion in prayer, His intimacy with the Father, and they were moved substantially by the warmth and reality of His prayer life. Out of all the things they could have asked, they focused on this: "Lord, teach us to pray" (Luke 11: 1).

We need to study the Lord's Prayer periodically and seek God's guidance on how to pray. Prayer is such a vital thing in our lives, the devil wants to give us wrong ideas about prayer. Prayer is a holy and sacred discipline, yet because of our fallen nature, we have the tendency to pervert the practice of prayer. For many, prayer becomes flippant and irreverent. For others, it's just a dull routine lacking life and warmth. Some people view prayer simply as a last resort; "if all else fails, we'll pray." In that way, prayer becomes a parachute, "I'm glad I have one, but I hope I don't have to use it." Others are just totally self-centered in prayer; viewing God as a big Santa Claus, they ramble off their big wish lists.

Prayer is so much more than that. We need the Lord's Prayer to cleanse our prayer lives and to help us get back on the right track. It really is a masterpiece of God's wisdom that all the elements of prayer would be encompassed and reduced to this little prayer of 66 words. This one little prayer gives us all the teaching we need on how to pray.

Isn't that amazing?

What do we do with the Lord's Prayer? There are two responses that the Lord's Prayer initiates.

> ## The Lord's Prayer is Used As:
>
> 1. A simple recitation
>
> 2. A model prayer upon which a rich devotional life can be developed

Simple Recitation

First, the Prayer is used as a simple recitation. We recite the Lord's Prayer because Jesus specifically instructs His disciples, "When you pray, say…" (Luke 11:2). Reciting the Lord's Prayer provides a sense of connection with the entire Christian community. Every Sunday morning, tens of thousands of churches all around the world stand and recite the Lord's Prayer. What a fellowship and dynamic we enter into!

In addition, we recite the Lord's Prayer because it is a perfect prayer that impacts our lives powerfully as we start a new week. God truly hears and answers the prayer, listening to each specification.

Finally, we recite the Lord's Prayer because it reminds us of the priorities, set forth by Jesus, as the objective of prayer. In doing this, we are protected and redirected from a lost focus in prayer.

When I was a boy, I took piano lessons because I desired to play in church. I wanted to play fast, exciting hymns (*Fly Fly Away*, *When We All Get to Heaven*, and so forth). I told Ruth Joplin, my instructor, to allow me to play these songs. My request was denied—she told me I needed to start with the scales. Over and over again, she made me repeat the scales until those tones and hand movements were second nature to me.

Through repetition, we learn. Reciting the Lord's Prayer over and over allows prayer to develop as a second nature. The elements of prayer are woven into the fabric of our souls and ingrained into the pattern of our thoughts.

A Model Prayer Upon Which a Rich Devotional Life Can Be Developed

Secondly, the Lord's Prayer is used as a model prayer upon which a rich devotional life can be developed. It is an outline to build upon, a skeleton upon which skin, muscle, and sinew are added. It directs us in fleshing out a beautiful life of prayer.

Do you ever feel perplexed when it comes to prayer? Do you ever feel like your prayer life is deficient? I think if we honestly evaluate our prayer lives, we may all feel like we're in kindergarten. Learning to pray should be a burning on our hearts.

There are seven elements of the Lord's Prayer I would like us to explore:

Elements of the Lord's Prayer

1. The Person We Address
2. The Posture We Assume
3. The Priority We Acknowledge
4. The Program We Advance
5. The Provision We Accept
6. The Protection We Access
7. The Praise We Articulate

The Person We Address

Isn't it wonderful we can call God Father? That was the favorite name Jesus had for God. He used it over two-hundred times. This was not just a formal address, it was a term of endearment similar to our "Daddy." It was **Abba**. Do you realize how revolutionary that was for Jesus to pray that way? You can study all the prayer literature on Judaism— and I mean there are tons of papers recording the prayers of Judaism—and nowhere do you find the invocation of God used in that manner. No Jew dared to call God "Father," and especially not **Abba!** And yet… Jesus did. Even better, He handed it down to us. Not only did He give us permission to do it, but He gave us the impulses to do it.

Galatians 4:4 states, "When the fullness of the time had come, God sent forth His Son, made of a woman, made under the law, to redeem those who were under the law, that we might receive the adoption of sons…" Since we've been set free from the law, we've been adopted into the family of God. "God has sent forth the Spirit of His Son into your hearts, crying 'Abba, Father!'" (Galatians 4:6 NKJV).

We can pray with such comfort, ease, and confidence because the person we address is indeed, "Our Father."

And let us not forget the "Our" word in the address, You are not an only child. God has a family and we are to remember our brothers and sisters when we pray. The entire prayer is employed with plural language.

The Posture We Assume

Locating the residence of our Father changes the complexion of the whole prayer, doesn't it? Heaven is His throne, and the earth is His footstool. He's the Heavenly Father, so even though there is this familiarity because of family, we maintain reverence by acknowledging His glory and greatness.

Think about some of the events on planet earth and the pomp and circumstance that surround these events that taken place on earth: award banquets, royal weddings in London, college graduations, the Olympics. Now multiply that by ten thousand times, and you still can't capture the majesty of His throne.

Time magazine back in the early 1960s had an image on the cover that captured the hearts of Americans. J. F. Kennedy was pictured in his office, sitting at his desk, talking on the phone. His two little children, John Jr. and Caroline, were playing with toys on the floor of the Oval Office. It was so captivating because these two diametrically opposed images bridged together. Here is the most powerful man in the free world, the President of the United States, sitting in his office working, and yet the children at his feet are comfortable and playful in his presence.

Oh, our great God embraces us with a beautiful ease, but He does not sacrifice His majesty in doing so— He is our Father, but our Heavenly Father.

The Priorities We Acknowledge

Do you know that the number one objective of prayer is for God to be glorified? Jesus said, "Ask and you shall receive so that the Father may be glorified in the Son" (John 15:7).

How you handle a name is indicative of how you feel about that person. You get a little bit annoyed if somebody forgets your name. As pastor of a wonderful church, I get tested at the door when I shake hands at the dismissal time. I try to remember everybody's name, but we have a large congregation and I'm getting too old and I do get a little confused sometimes. Some like to test me and tease me, "Pastor, what's my name?" I like to be playful with my responding, "At your age, you should know your name by now!"

All jokes aside, it hurts your feelings if someone forgets or mispronounces your name. Now, I don't take it personally if somebody calls me "Tim Woods," putting an S at the end of Wood. It's not my favorite thing, but I just respond, "I'm not a jungle, just a single tree." Ultimately, we would rather people pronounce our name properly. How you speak someone's name— the tone, pronunciation, and recollection— reveals your attitude toward that person.

People who are mishandling the name of God indicate that they have no reverence in their hearts for God. Our culture is filled with the blasphemy of God's name. Cursing takes the name of God and drags it into the mud. Combining God's name with other words defames and defiles it. How can people commit such atrocities? Because their hearts have no love for God or fear of God.

Therefore, this second component of the Lord's Prayer is actually a request! This is the first petition of the prayer and it asks God to help us treat His name with sacredness and reverence. It's not an assertion or a statement—"oh, our Father, who art in heaven, Your name is holy." No! it's a request! "God, let Your name be treated with sacredness. Let Your name be lifted up and given proper reverence." It's a request that the entirety of our lives would be defined by reverence for God.

That's how we start prayer; it is the very first petition. The greatest priority we acknowledge is that His name be glorified in our lives.

The Program We Advance

"Thy kingdom come, thy will be done on earth as it is in heaven..."

Did you know that we are partners with God in managing the universe? John Wesley said that "God will do nothing but in answer to prayer." I know God is sovereign—He has determined all things— but the same God who ordains the ends ordains the means. God uses the intercession of his people to accomplish His purposes, joining us in partnership with Him as He brings His kingdom into reality on earth.

The kingdom of God is not a realm, but a rule—it's the authority of Jesus Christ that destroys the works of the devil. The dispositional will of God is not always manifested in our earth, nor is the good nature of our God displayed in our world. There's a kingdom of darkness that challenges the kingdom of God and a spirit of rebellion and wickedness that rises up against the rule and will of God. I tell you, when we pray, we're in the warfare! When we pray, we are resisting the devil! When we pray, we're coming against the powers of darkness! When we pray, we're combating culture that is moving away from God. Prayer really does make a difference! It's not a meaningless exercise, but an efficient collaboration with God.

Jacob prayed, and his brother's angry heart, which was poisoned by twenty years of seeking revenge, was softened and reconciled. Abraham prayed as a 100-year-old man, and God enabled him to have a child. Joseph prayed, and God was able to take that which was evil and turn it into good. David prayed in the cave, and the evil designs of King Saul were frustrated. Esther prayed and fasted, and God used her and her cousin to preserve the people of God from the sinister attacks of wicked Haman. Daniel prayed, and he was able to interpret the dreams of the king and have an exalted ministry in three empires.

We could go on and on about how prayer changes the world, lives, families, and communities. We are partners with God as we pray for His will to be done! We pray, and the program of God's kingdom is advanced.

The Provision We Accept

"Give us this day our daily bread…"

Now I must admit, this petition is slightly deflating! The previous petitions place us on the top of the mountain where we breathlessly behold the glories of God. Praying about the name of God, the kingdom of God, and the will of God—we're on high ground, lifted into eternal, transcendent considerations. Whew!

But then—THUD! Our feet are placed back on the ground as we think about the food we put in our mouth. Really? We come down to earth to pray about carbohydrates? We're praying about bread on our table? How boring! Nonetheless, this petition reminds us that God truly cares about us. If we're not careful, we can view prayer in super-duper spiritual terms, but here we notice that God really cares about the food on our table, the clothes on our back, and the cars in our garage. He cares about our bills, our rent, and our financial burdens. He cares about our health, our healing, our mood, and our emotions. He cares about physical things— daily necessities!

Because God cares so deeply about us, we are liberated from a life of anxiety and stress. As we accept the provision of God, we are enabled to

133

rest peacefully in the knowledge that God will supply our every need.

The Pardon We Appropriate

"Forgive us our trespasses as we forgive those who trespass against us..."

Just as we need daily food, we need daily forgiveness. We're not perfect. Prayer is not about wearing a mask to impress God, but about being honest. He already knows all about you, anyway! Prayer is not about being like that Pharisee who prayed, "Oh God look how great I am." God didn't even listen to that man. He knows you're not great. On the other end of the spectrum, the despised Publican wouldn't even lift up his head, crying, "Oh Lord, be merciful to me, a sinner." He may not have returned home dignified, but he did go home justified.

Prayer is all about being honest. Sin gets into our lives, and we need to confess it daily by crying out for God's forgiveness. And the best part? Every time you confess your sins in prayer, He faithfully forgives you— every single time. He does!

Now, that doesn't mean you have to get re-saved every day. There's a difference between "judicial forgiveness" and "relational forgiveness." When you are saved, you receive "judicial forgiveness"—God legally pardons you, declares you righteous, and justifies you. This decision of the high court can never be overturned. "Who shall give anything to the charge of God's elect? It is God that justifies" (Romans 8:33). Judicial forgiveness is once and for all, settled and beautiful.

However, the justified ones still need what's called "relational forgiveness" because, as children of God, our fellowship with God gets strained. We build up barriers to the blessings of God, and the power of God can't flow fresh to us because junk gets collected in our lives. Every time we pray "God, forgive me," He renews our hearts with beautiful forgiveness, making our hearts tender and sweet.

134

You will be amazed at how merciful and faithful God will be to you when you confess your sins. Eventually, you will become so sweet that you desire to forgive others! If you're not forgiving others, something has gone terribly wrong—maybe you're not really receiving God's forgiveness.

A little brother and sister were fighting—making a real ruckus—so Daddy interrupted them and scolded them. Little Susie jumped up in Daddy's arms, saying, "I'm sorry Daddy, I'm sorry, forgive me for being bad, and having a bad attitude, and fighting like this, oh forgive me!" Daddy embraced his daughter and loved on her with kind words and kisses "I forgive you Baby, I forgive you, it's alright." She said, "I won't do it again." He replied, "I know, baby, I forgive you."

Then, while still holding her, he looked into the mirror to find his daughter leaning over Daddy's shoulder to stick her tongue out at her brother. He gently put her down and said, "Now darling, you can't be getting Daddy's forgiveness and at the same time sticking your tongue out at your brother."

As we receive the forgiveness of God for our own trespasses, we are enabled to express God's pardon to others.

The Protection We Access

"Lead us not into temptation but deliver us from evil..."

Even though God is faithful and forgiving, we must never get comfortable with sin. Sin dulls the ears and darkens the eyes. It devours the intellect and deceives the heart. It dwarfs the soul and diseases the body. My friends, you don't want sin in your life.

Part of our daily prayer life is for deliverance and protection—"Protect us Lord from the evil one! Lead us not into temptation!" You may say, "Well what does that mean? Does God sometimes lead us into temptation?" No. James Chapter 1 says that God never tempts you to do wrong things. Psalm 23 says that He leads us into paths of righteousness. What the prayer is actually seeking is for God's leadership to be so strong, convincing, and clear that any other path becomes undesirable to follow.

We ask that God's Spirit would pull us in the right direction and prevent us from distraction: "God, please lead me so I don't fall into temptation." When we access this heavenly protection through a daily commitment to prayer, we will be delivered from countless snares of the enemy. Some wonder why they keep falling into the traps of the devil. Do you have a daily discipline of prayer?

Three times Jesus told the disciples in the garden, "Wake up!" You can't just sleep in and have the victory. Wake up! Watch and pray that you enter not into temptation. The spirit is willing but the flesh is weak" (Matthew 26:41; paraphrase by author). The disciples slept instead of praying, and in that night of demonic pressure, they broke under the pressure and sinned. Oh I tell you, a life of prayer will deliver you from so much evil and harm. Through prayer, we are able to access the divine protection of God.

The Praise We Articulate

"For thine is the kingdom, the power, and the glory forever, amen."

Finally, the prayer comes full circle with a focus back on the glory of our God. We return to a God-focused life!

It's kind of funny, when you study the Lord's Prayer and all the commentaries— you can pile up 20 commentaries on the Lord's Prayer and all kind of notes on this prayer—but you will find very few lines commenting on the ending. The lack of attention to the ending of the prayer is kind of curious. I don't know why that is. In some manuscripts, the Bible doesn't even contain these last few words in the prayer, and that's why our brothers and sisters of the Catholic worship don't include this.

My mother and I once attended a Catholic funeral, and my mother had never attended Mass before. I was a little familiar with some of the routine, but she was not, so she felt like an outsider. She didn't understand when to sit, when to kneel, what to say, or what to do. She felt really out of it, but she wanted to participate. Finally, it was time to say the Lord's Prayer, and she perked up, "Well I know that!" Thankful to take part in the service, she cried out in a loud voice, "OUR FATHER WHO ART IN HEAVEN!"

She went on and on, not realizing that the church stops the prayer at "Deliver us from evil." But she kept going, and eventually she came to her great solo debut, "For thine is the kingdom, the power, and the..." Growing silent and red-faced, she whispered to me in embarrassment, "What's that about? Why did they stop the prayer?" I told her that the Catholic faith just stops the prayer at "Deliver us from the evil one." She thought that was quite silly, to recite an unfinished prayer! Well, it does sound somewhat like an unfinished prayer.

I like the way we have it in our King James Version because it really finishes out the prayer and brings us back to a focus on God. After all, focusing on God is the main objective of prayer—to erase all of the distractions, anxieties, worries, and irritations of life

We worship Him! We adore Him! As we seek first His kingdom and His righteousness first then we find that all our needs are met and we have nothing to worry about.

Are You Stuck?

I want to share a little story with you to demonstrate how the power of prayer can truly release God's blessings in your life. I know an executive of a large company, and hanging in his office is a print of a rowboat stuck in the sand. It's not very attractive or inspirational. If you just look at it from a distance, it's actually quite depressing!

This beautiful boat, built to be dancing on the waves, is stuck in the mud of the shoreline about 20 feet from the tide. The boat is constricted from fulfilling its purpose, too stuck to move and too heavy to be lifted. The executive *loves* to show this print to everyone, and they wonder why he has an image on his wall. How can that possibly be a motivator? The executive then directs them to the caption on the bottom of the print: "The tide always comes back."

During the executive's course in business, he went through a serious season of depression, professionally and personally. Resources dried up, and he became stuck! In an antique store one day, he saw the print and was encouraged by the words, "The tide always comes back." The picture gave him hope to go on, and he began to pray. And sure enough, the tide did come back! Blessings were restored!

Do you feel like you are *stuck,* and you don't know how to get unstuck? God is in charge of the tides. He can wash in with His presence and power, lifting you up and placing you right back where you need to be. He can release goodness in your life! Our job? Just pray a little bit. Let us be a prayerful church, and we will witness God's glory and restoration in our lives.

A JOYFUL CHURCH

A lady went to the doctor and she said, "My whole body is hurting. I'm not sure exactly what's going on, but every part of my body hurts." He said, "What do you mean?" She said, "Well, I'll show you." So she took her finger and touch her thigh and screamed. She took her finger touched her forearm and went "ouch." She took her finger and touched her neck and screamed some more. Finally the doctor said, "I know what's wrong with you. You have a broken finger." We all need a proper diagnosis.

I've been pastoring for many years and I've observed something – Christians are living defeated lives and they quit because they have broken joy. David prayed in Psalms 51, "Restore unto me the joy of your salvation." Your joy can become broken. When your joy is broken, you hurt all over. You become miserable and vulnerable to the attacks of the devil because you lack strength. Nehemiah gives us those famous words, "The joy of the Lord is your strength" (Nehemiah 8:10).

I had a friend who was teaching a summer Bible conference. One of his lectures was on the joy of Jesus. After the conference, a lady faced him in the corner of the building and just reamed him out. "That's a heretical teaching! Oh how dare you say Jesus had joy— He was a man of sorrows and acquainted with grief." And my friend said to her, "Yes ma'am, He was a man of sorrows and acquainted with grief and He sympathized with hurting people, and then of course on the cross He was supremely the man of sorrows and acquainted with grief. But He was also a man of joy!" He wanted to share the Scriptures with her about the joy of Jesus, but she just walked away triumphantly like she made her point.

There are a lot of Scriptures that talk about the joy of Jesus;

> Luke 10 reads that Jesus" rejoiced in the spirit" (Luke 10:21)

> In John 15 Jesus said to his disciples, "These things I have spoken to you that my Joy will be in you" (John 15:11).

If Jesus didn't manifest joy, then that would have been perplexing to the disciples. For Him to say, "I'm speaking to you so that my joy will be in you" – that means His joy was conspicuous! It was obvious and evident. He said," I want my joy to be in you."

> Then in John 17, Jesus expressed desire that He wanted the joy that was in Him to be fulfilled in His followers (John 17:13).

> Hebrew 2:2 tells us that Jesus endured the cross because of the joy that was set before Him. Jesus was a man of joy. He really was.

In fact, Psalms 45:7 tells us that Messiah would have the oil of gladness above His fellows. That means when Jesus was in a particular spot, He was the happiest person there. You couldn't *out-happy* Jesus. You couldn't *out-joy* Jesus. At every party, He had gladness above anybody else that was in that room. If we want to be true followers of Christ, we have to think about joy. We need to identify the source of joy and we need to draw deeply from those wells.

What Gives Us Joy?
1. God's Sovereignty
2. God's Supply
3. God's Service
4. God's Scripture
5. God's Sanctuary

God's Sovereignty

"Rejoice in the Lord always. Again I will say, rejoice!" –
Philippians 4:4

You can't always rejoice in your circumstances. You can't always rejoice in the conditions of your life. Sometimes your body doesn't feel well. Sometimes people are against you. Sometimes things are tough. But you can always rejoice in the Lord, because He is always the same.

You may ask, "Did Paul practice what he preached?" Paul did! When he wrote this book of Philippians, he was in jail. How could he have joy? His feet were itching because he had a fire in his bosom to run and fulfill his call to preach to the gentiles. It was so burdensome for him to be confined and cramped in that dungeon. But at that time of great stress, Paul had abounding joy!

He was in prison for preaching the gospel. How could he have joy even there? Because he believed that God was in control. Paul testified, "My imprisonment has worked out for the furtherance of the gospel. I had it in my mind how to further the gospel. I wanted to be free. But because of my chains, other people are getting more bold in proclaiming the gospel. And the propagation of the gospel is now expanding and enlarging. I'm bound, but the Word of God is not bound. I just rejoice that Christ is preached. I don't always have to be the one in the pulpit. I don't always have to always be the one on the platform. I rejoice because God is working even in this situation" (my paraphrase of Philippians 1:12-16).

God's Supply

"Until now you have asked nothing in My name. Ask, and you will receive, that your joy may be full."
— John 16:24

My grandmother, Minnie Reynolds, was a prayer warrior. She was an Assemblies of God evangelist. God used her mightily because she was a praying woman. It was her custom to rise at 5am and seek God on her knees with an open Bible before her. And then my mother took her place as a prayer warrior. She picked up that mantle from her mother. Then I learned to pray from my mother. From the time I was a child, I learned the value of prayer and carved out time to seek God in the privacy of my home or on the path that cut through the woods of my neighborhood.

I found it a pleasure to tarry in God's presence with a spirit of praise and petition. I also learned the value of short prayers and emergency prayers. Like Peter when he was going down in the stormy sea, "Lord save me!" He didn't have time to recite the Lord's Prayer. Those 66 words would have sunk him. He had to quickly cry out, "Lord save me." An emergency prayer is efficacious. "God, you're a present help in the time of trouble, help me right now." Life becomes enriched and empowered when we develop consistent habits and live in a spirit of unceasing prayer. The joy of watching God work so skillfully in answer to prayer, becomes such a thrilling adventure.

I was seventeen years old and had just finished my first year of Bible College. I was now home for the summer. I had just got home and received a phone call from Pastor Joe McCoy, who pastored a Church of God in Swainsboro, Georgia. He said, "I want you to come and be my associate pastor for the summer before you start your sophomore year at the University. I know a lot of churches in the area to supplement more of your income; you can go out and preach revivals all summer and at the same time work with me in my local church."

I was excited at the invitation, my first job in the ministry! But I didn't have a car. Mom and dad had invested their extra money into my college expenses and did not have the resources to purchase a car. It was early in the afternoon and I said to my mother, "I don't have a car. I have no savings. I don't know how to get to Georgia. I didn't know how to travel around to all these revivals."

My mother said, "Why don't we just pray?" She got on her knees in the living room and I joined her in a season of prayer. One hour after the prayer meeting my dad arrived at the house and he knew nothing of the situation that we just prayed over. To my surprise, he walked in with the keys to a beautiful little tan Volkswagen bug. My dad said to me, "The funniest thing just happened. I was just talking to my mechanic friend David, and he had this Volkswagen that he's been working on. It is very nice. He just put four new tires on it. For some reason we were just talking about you being in Bible College and how God is using you. David decided he wanted to share this car with you."

I took hold of the keys and ran out front to see my first car. There was such joy in my heart, not just because the need was met, but because I had just experienced an expression of God's love and care. It felt wonderful to know that God was thinking about me and actually hearing my prayers.

God's Service

"Serve the LORD with gladness; Come before His presence with singing." – Psalms 100:2

God asked Moses, "What is that in your hand" (Exodus 3)? What a probing question. I want ask you that question. "What do you have in your hand? What gifting do you have?" Let's not be like Moses and make excuses. Moses said, "All I have is a stick and a stutter." God said "I'll take what you have and I'll use it but with my power." Moses launched into a 40 year ministry that was saturated with manifestations of God's glory. For the first 40 years of his life while living in the affluence of Egypt, he thought he was a "somebody." The next 40 years of his life, serving as a simple shepherd in the backside of the desert, he learned that he was a "nobody." Then the last 40 years of his life, as the emancipator and prophetic leader of God's people, he discovered what God can do with a "nobody." We will not have depths of joy until we discover God's assignment, develop His gifting in us and then release His anointing through faithful service.

Paul tells us repeatedly to serve the Lord with the right motivation and attitude. It's not enough to just serve the Lord and then act like a martyr. Some volunteer for ministry and then act like it is so painful. They want to let everyone know how much they are suffering. We are to serve the Lord with gladness (Psalms 100:2).

That's not just for the greeters of the church. You know greeters, they have to put on the smile and serve with gladness or they're contradicting what greeting is all about. It doesn't matter whether you are a greeter, a Sunday School teacher or you fill another position, we are to serve the Lord with gladness and there is always joy in doing something for our wonderful Lord.

I have a friend who is a retired surgeon. He has been blessed with wealth and doesn't just live in the lap of luxury thinking about the wonderful career and amenities he has enjoyed. This precious man goes once a year to a medical clinic in a third world country and exercises his skills to help people who are less advantaged and he does it free of charge. He said, "I do it because I want to help them. Love is motivating me; I care and I also do it for me because I couldn't find any comfort in just having cars and cable TV. I need to do something for God."

Don't you feel that way? Don't you want joy? Joy can always be found when involved in God's service.

God's Scripture

"The statutes of the LORD are right, rejoicing the heart; The commandment of the LORD is pure, enlightening the eyes." – Psalm 19:8

Hebrews 11:35 tells us that there is pleasure in sin, but that pleasure is only for a season. The world has things to offer and they advertise really big. The advertisement are bigger than the delivery. The world will present some pleasurable experiences, but nothing can compare with the spiritual reality God provides. The world can't compete with the joy of God's people as they search the Scriptures and mine the wealth of divine revelation. Romans 12:2 "Be not conformed to this world, but be transformed by the renewing of your mind, that you may prove what is the good and acceptable and prefect will of God."

Devouring the Word of God is like a hungry, weary traveler sitting down at a beautiful Thanksgiving banquet. Think about such a famished traveler sitting down at a feast and enjoying. That's the joy we're talking about, because the Bible is described as spiritual food. It is like a loaf of bread, "Man should not live by bread alone, but by every word that proceeds from the mouth of God" (Matthew 4:4). The Word of God is like the delicious protein of meat. Hebrews 5:12-14 instructs us to grow strong teeth and molars so we can masticate and digest the Word of God. The Bible is like unto milk according to I Peter 2:2 and honey in Psalms

19:10. Can you make a meal out of bread, milk, meat and honey? I think you can but so many Christians have never pulled up a chair to partake of that feast and yet wonder why they have no joy.

God's Sanctuary

"When I remember these things, I pour out my soul within me. For I used to go with the multitude; I went with them to the house of God, With the voice of joy and praise, With a multitude that kept a pilgrim feast." – Psalms 42:4

Entering into God's sanctuary is the most important thing we do during the week and I don't say that lightly. The most important thing we do in the week is the Sunday morning act of worship because everything we are and everything we do, must flow out of worship. If we don't have a worship experience, it's like a car without fuel; and a garden without sunshine. We have to abide in the vine (John 15). Without Christ we can do nothing. It is possible to be busy and yet barren. A fruitful life is produced from a branch that is residing and resting in the virtues and vitalities of the vine. We need to get into His presence and worship.

Some people want to complain that worship is dull and boring. Maybe the fault is with the worshipper who might be dull and boring. Seven times the Bible warns us about being dull of hearing. Worship will become dull and dry if we lose the sensitivity of hearing. When we come to church, do we hear the voice of the Spirit? Do we hear the voice of the Spirit in the prayer? Do we hear the voice of the Spirit in the reading of Scripture? Do we hear the voice of the Spirit in all the anthems, songs and preaching? Someone said to me, "Pastor you're preaching over my head." I replied, "Then ask God to raise up your head."

I was attending a leadership conference where the speaker showed a 30 second video. He said, "I want you to watch how many times the people in white clothes pass the ball." The video showed this big gym with all these people playing basketball. And several were dressed in white. About 40 of us were at the conference and we all were staring at this video, counting how many times those in white threw the ball. I came up with about 16 in white who were throwing the ball. And the correct answer was 17, so I was close. Others had counted 10 and some had counted 20. So we got into this big discussion about how many times did those dressed in white pass the ball.

Then the leader asked this, "How many saw the huge gorilla in the gym?" We didn't see any gorilla. Nobody saw the gorilla! The leader played the video again and sure enough, there was a big gorilla! We aren't talking about a poodle dog. We are talking about a gorilla that walked into the gym, stood there and then walked out without being seen. Why? Because we were focused on one thing and could not see what was very plain and obvious. The video was illustrating a principle called "selective attention." This principle means that we choose to give attention to one item and that intense focus can eclipse everything else that is in plain view. I would love for people to come to church on Sunday morning with "selective attention." Our worship experience would be so much more meaningful if would put such a laser focus on God that nothing could distract us.

Oh, we must train ourselves to worship. It's not automatic. We must be deliberate and determined to enter into worship and open up to the lovely presence of the Lord.

God's Strength

"The LORD is my light and my salvation; Whom shall I fear? The LORD is the strength of my life; Whom shall I be afraid?" – Psalms 27:1

Fear can steal all your joy. Looking at Psalm 27:6! We read, "And now my head will be lifted up above my enemies around me, and I will offer in His tent sacrifices with shouts of joy; I will sing, yes, I will sing praises to the Lord."

Have you ever been bullied? Nadin Khoury was a little 13-year-old boy from Liberia, a war torn country. With his mother, they escaped and came to America. Working as a maid at a hotel in Minnesota didn't work out well, so they moved to Philadelphia. She was unemployed and couldn't get work. Khoury was prime picking for the seven bullies who beat him, called him names and said derogatory things about his dear mother. Finally, He was attacked, dragged through snow, shoved in a tree and hung from a fence. Thankfully, a kind person came along and rescued him.

This incident was caught on video which got to the police and the bullies were arrested. The story hit the local news and from there it went to the nationwide morning show called The View. Here is what happened for little Nadin Khoury. He was interviewed on the program showing the video of him being beat up by those boys. He tried to look brave but his bottom lip quivered. He said with tears in his eyes, "You know, there are some boys that are smaller than I am and we need to stop this kind of behavior."

The producer had a surprise for little Nadin Khoury. Three big guys came on the show from the Philadelphia Eagles. Little Nadin Khoury was an avid fan of the Eagles and these three famous football players sat down with him on the stage. DeSean Jackson pulled out his jersey and signed it for little Nadin Khoury. Then DeSean Jackson said, "Nadin, I'm giving you my personal cell phone number. If anybody ever bothers you again, I'm on speed dial. These two linebackers and I will be to you in 10 minutes to take care of whatever battle you have. You don't have to worry about anything. We are going to be your personal bodyguards." Nadin Khoury never worried about getting bullied with three football players from the Eagles as his personal bodyguards!

I don't know what kind of problems you have at school, home or work. I don't know what kind of enemies gang up against you too apply pressure and push you into fear. But I know this, the Lord is your bodyguard and the Lord fights your battles. David said, "The Lord is my light and my salvation; whom shall I fear? The Lord is the strength of my life; whom shall I be afraid?"

A GIVING CHURCH

1 Corinthians 16:1-2

Now concerning the collection for the saints, as I have given orders to the churches of Galatia, so you must do also: on the first day of the week let each one of you lay something aside, storing up as he may prosper, that there be no collections when I come.

Two men crashed in their private plane on an island in the South Pacific. Both survived. One of the men brushed himself off and proceeded to run all over the island to see if they had any chance of survival. When he returned, he rushed to his friend and screamed, "The island is uninhabited. There is no food or water. We are going to die!"

The other man leaned back against a tree, folded his arms, and said with a smile, "I'm not worried, I make $100,000 a month." The first man grabbed his friend and shook him, "Listen, we are on an uninhabited island. No food, no water… we are going to die!" The other man, unruffled, again responded, "We will not die. I make $100,000 a month." Mystified, the first man yelled, "For the last time, I'm telling you, we are doomed. NOT INHABITED! NO FOOD! NO WATER!" Still unfazed, the friend replied, "Listen, I make over $100,000 a month. I am a faithful tither to my local church. That means I give 10 percent of my income to the church. Believe me, my pastor will find us."

Church leaders are concerned about financial support of the church, but the main objective of this sermon is not to increase the income of this church. That is always a desire, because the more we have, the more we can do for God. My main concern is that you enjoy the fullness that God has purposed for you.

I am cautious to preach on prosperity, because I know this teaching has been abused by so many pulpits. I am not a prosperity preacher, but I am not a poverty preacher. We need balance. Here are three things to keep in mind.

First of all, we need to understand that sometimes our faith will be tested with a season of famine and hardship. Genesis 12:10 tells us there was a famine in the Land of Promise. Wow! You can claim promises and meet conditions to fulfill those promises and still face a season of famine.

Second, we must recognize that some Christians will be selected by God to undergo a severe persecution that will involve the reduction of income. This happened to the church of Smyrna as described in Revelations 2. As a result of their testimony for Christ, they were excluded from the guilds and the worker's unions. Thus, they could not get gainful employment. "I know your works, tribulation and poverty…" (Revelation 2:9a). They suffered deep poverty because of their faith.

Third, we must recognize that the greatest blessings of God are spiritual, not material. Let us not surrender to the superficial mindset of our contemporary culture in thinking that more stuff can satisfy the soul.

With these three recognitions in mind, we seek to find balance in our theology of prosperity. Paul tells us that a life of godliness is profitable for this world and for the one to come (I Timothy 4:8). When we follow God's plan for financial management by seeking out His wisdom, surely blessings will follow.

So, let me ask a few questions…

➢ Have you made God your financial partner?

➢ Is your pocketbook converted?

What a terrible error to exclude God from our personal finances. God cares about our financial stress, job satisfaction, monthly bills, desires, needs and necessities. Jesus said, "Seek first the Kingdom of God and His righteousness and all these things shall be added unto you" (Matthew 6:33).

What is God's wisdom concerning personal finances? Let's survey the Bible and make a simple list:.

Biblical Financial Principles

1. Priority of Stewardship
2. Practicality of Work
3. Pursuit of Investments
4. Prudence of Savings
5. Patience in Spending
6. Principle of Generosity
7. Perspective of Eternity
8. Passion of Worship

Priority of Stewardship

"Will a man rob God? Yet you have robbed Me! But you say, 'In what way have we robbed You?' In tithes and offerings. Bring all the tithes into the storehouse, that there may be food in my house. And try Me now in this," says the Lord of hosts. "If I will not open for you the windows of heaven and pour out for you such blessing that there will not be room enough to receive it." – Malachi 3:8, 10

A college professor was teaching his class one day, and he asked the student in the front row to lend him a pencil for a moment. When he received the pencil, he immediately broke it in half. The reaction of the class was one of shock and disgust. They cried out, "What right do you have to break someone else's pencil?" The teacher proceeded to explain that it was actually his pencil. He had planted the pencil with that student before class started. When the class learned that, all the disgust was gone.

Why? Since the pencil actually belonged to the professor, the class knew he maintained the right to do whatever he pleased with it.

Some people are outraged when God demands that His people give up a portion of their income and bring it to the temple in a spirit of worship. Why? Because they have the idea that they own their stuff! "This is my money!" they exclaim. But when we understand the biblical perspective of stewardship, that God owns everything, and we are merely stewards of His gifts, then that changes everything. He has a right to demand we worship Him with the presentation of financial gifts.

Our giving to God must be a priority. Moses said that God is the one who gives us power to get wealth (Deuteronomy 8:18). James declares, "Every good gift and perfect gift is from above and cometh down from the Father of lights with whom there is no variableness or shadow of turning" (James 1:17). Therefore, our Sunday morning participation in the collection is a reminder that every blessing comes from God, of which we are called to be good stewards.

Practicality of Work

"Do not sleep lest you come to poverty; open your eyes and you shall be satisfied with bread." – Proverbs 20:13

Work is not a four letter word. Someone said, "I'm looking for a formula that works." Stop looking! The formula *is* work! Examine some wisdom from the book of Proverbs regarding work:

➢ *"In all labor there is profit, but idle chatter leads only poverty." – Proverbs 14:23*

➢ *"The lazy man will not plow because of winter; he will beg during harvest and have nothing." – Proverbs 20:4*

➢ *"He who tills his hand will have plenty of bread, but he who follows frivolity*

Pursuit of Investments

"Cast your bread upon any waters, for you will find it after many days. Give a serving to seven, and also to eight, for you do not know what evil will be on the earth."

— Ecclesiastes 11:1-2

Solomon was a wise man who knew about investments. What does he mean when he says, "Cast bread on water?" Doesn't sound particularly inviting—sounds like you will get soggy bread! The explanation for this statement can be found in another part of the Bible:

"For the king had merchant ships at sea with the fleet of Hiram. Once every three years the merchant ships came bringing gold, silver, ivory, apes, and monkeys. So King Solomon surpassed all the kings of the earth in riches and wisdom." – 1 Kings 10:22-23

Solomon was a trader and investor! He bought ships and sent them out. They would stay out sometimes three years and they would return with great profit and riches. Maybe that is where we got the phrase, "When your ship comes in."

General Patton used to say, "I never want it to be said, 'We are holding. We are holding the fort and holding our ground.' No! The only thing we should be holding is the enemy. We must be advancing. Moving forward!" This is the attitude we should have with our finances; taking our resources and making bold ventures to multiply what God has entrusted to us.

While I am not trained in the investment department, there are many companies and investment agents who can competently give beneficial counsel with those matters.

Proverbs speaks of the importance of seeking wise counsel for the different compartments of our lives.

> ➤ *"He who walks with wise men will be wise, but the companion of fools will be destroyed." – Proverbs 13:20*

> ➤ *"Without counsel plans go awry, but in the multitude of counselors they are established." – Proverbs 15:22*

A warning for the wise: we must conquer greed and avoid any "get rich quick" schemes. Proverbs 28:22 states, "A man with an evil eye hastens after riches, and does not consider that poverty will come upon him." If a financial project sounds too good to be true—it might be!

Notice that Solomon also instructs us to explore diversification. "Give a serving to seven and also to eight." In other words, "Don't put all your eggs in one basket." Invest in several projects. Put some here and there. Spread it out.

Finally, and most importantly, be sure to pray about all your investment choices. Proverbs 3:5-6 shows us the need to apply prayer to every aspect of our lives, "Trust in the Lord with all your heart, and lean not on your own understanding; in all your ways acknowledge Him, and He shall direct your paths."

When I was a child, my mom and dad got excited about a business adventure. They were invited to join another family in buying a Western Auto store in Cambridge, Maryland. They decided to quit their steady jobs and put all their savings into this store.

Before going through with the deal, Mom and Dad went to the Eastern Shore for a church conference. Dad went to church that night, but Mom stayed in the motel because she was so excited about the move. She was looking at the real estate section of the newspaper to find a new place to live.

However, when Dad got back to the motel from the church service, he said to my mom, "We are not going to invest in this store. God spoke to me in worship tonight and warned me against it." Mom obliged. They went back home and obeyed the leading of the Spirit. The other family pursued the store, and within one year it went bankrupt. They lost everything.

God wants to be your financial partner! Don't look at God as one who wants to interfere with your money and reduce you to misery. He knows how to prosper and protect you and your finances.

Prudence of Savings

"The ants are a people not strong, yet they prepare their food in the summer." – Proverbs 30:25

This Bible verse is telling us something so basic and obvious, "Get ready—winter will come!" We also use the phrase, "Saving for a rainy day." We need to buy insurance. We need a retirement plan. We need money set aside for emergencies and lean seasons. Some get super spiritual with the attitude, "I don't need a safety net; I'll just trust God." I like what they said in the Civil War, "Trust God, but keep powder dry."

We need to be responsible! It is not living in faith to be reckless. The devil tempted Jesus to jump off the roof of the temple, forcing God to rescue Him with angelic intervention. Jesus would not give in to that kind of foolish presumption. He basically told the devil, "I'm not jumping off the roof when God gave me a flight of steps to walk down."

Faith and prudence are qualities that need to be balanced. We are not to live in fear and obsessively stockpile, but we are to put a little back. Faith and prudence are not in competition; they are in cooperation.

Patience in Spending

Luke 29:19 "In patience, possess your souls."

I enjoy shopping! Others prefer to shop online, but I like going to the store to enjoy the experience. When it comes to spending, however, restraint must be exercised. We need that fruit of the Spirit called *self-control.* If we are not careful, we can find ourselves in trouble financially.

What is displayed in the store windows can be so alluring and walking through the stores with a credit card can give us the idea that we can accumulate things without actually paying for them.

Now I'm not against credit cards because in our cashless society, we need them to function. You can't even rent a car without a credit card! However, we can get trapped into impulsive spending habits without truly counting the cost.

The other day I got a pre-approved credit card in the mail. Immediately, I began to praise God, "Thank you, Lord!" I thought it was a gift from God, so I proceeded to share the blessing with my friend. I said, "Look, this store sent me a card. They said they like me! They believe in me! They trust in me! I want to personally thank them by going there and buying a bunch of stuff." My friend quietly responded, "That credit card might not be from the Lord. It might be from the devil. You might want to take some scissors and perform plastic surgery."

In America, $25 of every $100 are consumer debt. That is twenty-five percent! Proverbs 22:7 explains the true dynamic of consumer debt, "The rich rules over the poor, and the borrower is servant to the lender." If you buy a dinner for $25 and put it on a charge card, do you know how much that dinner will cost you if you pay minimum monthly payments? It will cost *$50.* Use credit cards as a tool of convenience, but be careful with it.

We must be patient in spending and discern between "saving" and "spending." I came home one day with joy and said to my daughter,

"Look how smart I am! I bought this new suit. It was regularly priced at $400, but it was marked down to $200. I saved $200!" She responded, "No! You didn't save $200, you *spent* $200"! Ouch!

Nothing is wrong with spending and shopping; that is one of the joys of life. However, we must stay within our budgets and resist all the pressure of manipulative advertising. You can be sexy without that special toothpaste. You can look young without that amazing shampoo. You can be successful without that incredible sweater. We must have patience in spending—saving for some things and saying "no" to other things.

Principle of Generosity

"There is one that scatters and yet increases and there is he who withholds more than is necessary and it tends to poverty."
Proverbs 11:24

"He who sows sparingly will also reap sparingly, and he who sows generously will also reap generously." – II Corinthians 9:6

R. G. Letourneau was an inventor of earth-moving machines and he got to the place where he gave 90 percent of his income to God in various ways. Miraculously, he kept increasing and prospering! One day he was asked the secret of his success. He replied, "I shovel out the money and God shovels it back to me—but God has a bigger shovel."

Let your lifestyle be one of generosity. In your tipping at the restaurant—be generous. When you see a homeless person on the side of the road—be generous. With your children – be generous. When you go out with friends—offer to pay. Throw money around. It is glorious how it turns around to bless you. Actually, it is miraculous! Luke 6:38 describes the miracle involved in giving, "Give, and it shall be given to you; good measure, pressed down, shaken together, and running over will be put into your bosom."

Perspective of Eternity

Jesus does not tell us to avoid storing up treasures! He just tells us not to store our treasures in the wrong place! He is concerned about poor investments. If all your money and materialism are wrapped up in planet earth and this temporal life, you are investing in the wrong bank. Riches are very uncertain.

A few years ago we suffered a recession and discovered that a downturn in the economy can rob us of a big chunk of our financial worth and precious savings. No earthly treasure is safe, so Jesus tells us to invest in eterty. When we sacrifice earthly gain for heavenly values, we will one day enjoy eternal rewards.

Take a look at some quotes from people who understood the value of eternal investment:

> ➢ *"I value all things only by the price they shall gain in eternity."* – *John Wesley*

> ➢ *"I place no value on anything I have or may possess, except in relation to the kingdom of God."* – *David Livingstone*

> ➢ *"He is no fool who gives what he cannot keep to gain what he cannot lose."* – *Jim Elliot*

> ➢ *"Whatever good thing you do for Him, if done according to His Word, is laid up for you as treasure in chests and coffers, to be brought out to be rewarded before both men and angels, to your eternal comfort."* – *John Bunyan*

Passion of Worship

"Honor the Lord with your possessions, and the first fruits of your increase." — Proverbs 3:9

A poor young lady was attending a missionary conference, and she was moved by the appeal to give in support of world missions. She felt bad because she had no money to give. Then she thought of a very expensive and precious gold ring that she wore, it was the only thing of value she owned. With joy she took the ring off her finger and placed it in the offering plate.

When the ushers counted the offering, they saw this ring and told the pastor about it. The pastor knew where this ring came from and was moved by the sacrifice of the young lady. Knowing how precious the ring was to the young lady, he decided to return it to her. When he tried to return the ring, however, she resisted. "Pastor, you can't give that ring back to me," she said. "Why can't I give it back to you?" he asked. She responded, "Because I didn't give it to you. I gave it to Jesus, and only He can give it back."

When we include God in our finances, we discover such joy and, at the same time, the church is empowered to fulfill the vision entrusted to her.

AN IMPACTFUL CHURCH

In the 1980s, the Chicago Bears was a celebrated Super Bowl team. Their coach was Mike Ditka and they had a star player by the name of Refrigerator Perry. At a pre-game devotional, the chaplain asked the Frig to say the Lord's Prayer. The quarterback, Jim McMahon, leaned over to the chaplain and whispered in his ear, "I bet you $50 he does not know the Lord's Prayer."

It is kind of odd that they would make a bet over the Lord's Prayer, but the chaplain said, "Alright. You are on." The Fridge began to pray, "Now I lay me down to sleep.." Jim McMahon shook his head, handed the money over to the chaplain and said, "Bummer, I thought for sure he would not know the Lord's Prayer."

I am glad we know the Lord's Prayer because we say it every Sunday. And that second petition is so meaningful, "Thy Kingdom Come."

There are two missional assignments given to the church today. The primary mission of the church is to save souls. Get people ready for heaven! But the secondary mission of the church is to bring some heaven down to earth and thus manifest the kingdom of God. The kingdom of God is the realm of God's rule. It is the arena where God exercises and executes His blessed will. We pray, "Thy kingdom come, thy will be done on earth as it is in heaven."

Things are not doing so well in the kingdom of men—in the kingdoms of this world. Terrorism, violence, pilots drowning planes, massacres in Kenya, poverty, starving children, broken hearts, broken families!

Jesus came and said, "Repent, the kingdom is at hand." I am come to bring "up there" — "down here." The gospel is not just about getting people ready to get "out of here and go up there."

Remember *Star Trek*? When members of the team were in trouble down in some weird planet of the universe, they would pray to a guy named Scotty, "Beam me up Scotty." Yes, the gospel gives us power to get beamed up from here to up there. But there is another prayer and passion we must have. "Up there" needs to come "down here." Thy kingdom come, thy will be done.

The visible church manifests the spiritual kingdom of God. As we do the work of the gospel in preaching, administration of the sacraments, offering up of praise and prayers –then people are filled with the grace of God. When people are saturated with the grace of God, they will go forth and make an impact on our contemporary culture. Jesus said to His followers, "You are the salt of the earth, the light of the world" (Matthew 5:13-14). So the church is in the soul saving business and in that pursuit of evangelism we improve and upgrade society. "Up there" is coming "down here."

In the first century, many pious Jews longed for the kingdom of God to come. They were weary with Caesar on the throne and Rome ruling. They longed for the kingdom of God to triumph. But there were different ideas of how that would come to pass. There were three different groups in Israel that had distinct strategies and philosophies on how the kingdom would come. All three strategies were wrong and Jesus showed each group a better way – God's way. We need to hear this. These three faulty strategies are still popular today. But Jesus shows us how to get "up there" — "down here."

The Zealots: Radical Revolution

The first group who longed for the kingdom of God was the zealots. What was there strategy? Radical Revolution.

They were an extreme nationalistic party who determined to overthrow the Romans using force and violence. They were freedom fighters, or terrorists, depending on your politics. That's why initially they got so excited about Palm Sunday. Often we think of Palm Sunday as an innocent children's parade. But it was not! Palms were symbols of Jewish nationalism.

During two major wars against Rome, Israelite rebels illegally minted coins and put palm branches on them. The palm branch was a political symbol. Waiving a palm branch in front of Rome was like waving a red flag in front of a bull. It was a declaration of war. The triumphal entry was, for the zealots, a military statement. What did they shout? "Hosanna, blessed is He who comes in the name of the Lord." Hosanna – save us now. In other words, "Blessed is our new King, save us now, save us from Pilate, save us from Herod, save us from Caesar. Crush Rome and liberate us." These were fighting words.

But Jesus would not fight. One of the primary differences between Jesus and Mohammed is the Mohammed was a military leader. Jesus would not fight Rome. And so the Hosannas hushed. The excited crowd disappeared. Before the week was over, Jesus took up a cross, walked the via Delarosa, and He surrendered Himself to the death of crucifixion. God's plan for victory was sacrificial love.

Jesus had offended the Zealots prior to this. They did not like it when Jesus taught, "If anyone forces you to go one mile, then go with them two miles" (Matthews 41:5). That was a direct reference to the law that the Romans had in place. If a Roman soldier was traveling with his back pack and decided he wanted a little break, he could grab a Jew from off the street and say, "You carry my baggage for one mile." Oh, how the Jews hated that law. What a burden! What a humiliation! What an inconvenience!

But Jesus talked about sacrificial love. He said, "If a soldier insists you go on mile. Then after you have walked a mile and reached the limit of the law, then tell the solider, "You know, I want to walk one more mile for you. I appreciate your work as a soldier. I want to be a blessing to you. The first mile, the law said I had to carry your burden. But now I want to carry your burden, not in law, but because of love."

Jesus taught sacrificial love and then demonstrated it. He bore that burden of the cross all the way to the top of mount Calvary. The Zealots were wrong. The Kingdom does not come through violence – but through voluntary love.

The Sadducees: Cowardly Compromise

But then there was a second group that had a specific strategy for bringing forth the kingdom of God. This group was the Sadducees. What was there strategy? Cowardly Compromise!

They decided to assimilate. They looked at the Romans and figured, "If you can't beat 'em, join 'em." They worked with tax collectors and paid allegiance to Caesar. So they took the philosophy, "When in Rome, do as the Romans do." They even wanted to be popular with their teaching content. And so they forsook the old truths of orthodoxy to embrace the philosophies of modernity. They did not believe in angels or the resurrection or miracles. I guess that is why they were Sad - u see? They were all about fitting into the world. New morals! New theology! New liturgy! We must appeal to the world!

But Jesus made it clear that God's way is not compromise with the kingdoms of this world. One day Jesus was asked this question, "Teacher...we know you are a man of integrity and that you teach the way of God in accordance with truth. You are not swayed by others. Tell us then, what is your opinion? Is it right to pay the imperial tax to Caesar or not?" (Matthew 22:16-17).

That was a tricky question. If Jesus answered the question with a "yes," people would hate Him for giving in to Rome. If He said "no," Rome would be arresting Him. Jesus said, "Show me a coin used for paying taxes. Whose image is on the coin?" They replied, "Caesar." Jesus said, "Give to Caesar what belongs to Caesar and give to God what belongs to God" (Matthew 22:19-21).

What wisdom and balance! Yes, we cooperate with the kingdoms of this world. We render that which belongs to Caesar. We cooperate. We pay taxes. We obey laws. We show patriotic loyalty. We honor the king. We give to Caesar what belongs to Caesar. We cooperate, but we do not compromise. Because we give to God what belongs to God.

There are things that do not belong to Caesar. The right to direct and dictate worship does not belong to Caesar. The claim of ultimate allegiance does not belong to Caesar. The defining of morals does not belong to Caesar. The source of hope does not belong to Caesar. The nourishment of the soul does not belong to Caesar. The administration of the affairs of the church does not belong to Caesar. The definition of marriage does not belong to Caesar. The gospel message does not belong to Caesar.

The claims of the kingdoms of this world are limited. Each individual has a conscience, and that conscience is to be a little sanctuary, a little chapel. No earthly king has the right to invade that small sanctuary. No king is to claim authority that belongs to God alone. There are things that do not belong to Caesar.

Some of the emperors of Rome would get upset when Christians would not pay homage to the throne of the Rome. Nero persecuted Christians because he was simply morally insane. He was Dr. Evil. But Marcus Aurelius was an emperor who was applauded for his high morals and reasonable reign. And yet he was one of the worse persecutors of the church. Why? Because he saw Christians as a threat to the security and glory of the Roman Empire.

Christians would not give to Rome the ultimate devotion. They would not say that "Caesar is Lord" and they would not call Rome and eternal city. Aurelius condemned Christians for being unpatriotic. But Christians were not troublemakers. They simply held the conviction that there are some things that do not belong to Caesar. They would not say that

"Caesar is Lord" –they stood tall and confessed, "Jesus is Lord." And they would not say that Rome is the eternal city –they would sing, "Here we have no continuing city but we seek one to come." We have another version of that song, "This world is not my home, I'm only passing through."

They cooperated with Rome, but they made spiritual worship their ultimate priority. In that worship experience, Hebrews 12 tells us that we climb Mount Zion and in that ascent we transcend the empires of this world. "Therefore, since we are receiving a kingdom which cannot be shaken, let us have grace, by which we may worship God acceptably with reverence and godly fear. For our God is a consuming fire" (Hebrews 13:28-29).

The Sadducees were wrong. The way to manifest the kingdom of God is not worldliness—it is worship.

The Essenes: Religious Retreat

Then there was a third group that longed for the Kingdom of God. This was the Essenes. They had a specific strategy. Their idea was religious retreat.

Oh, they were determined to be responsible for the coming of the Kingdom. They said, "Let's seek holiness. Let us piously drop out of society. Let us give up on this world. Let us withdraw, climb in caves, protect our holy robes from the corruption of society, and wait for the coming of Christ."

They were cave men. They lived in the caves of the deserts of Israel. They lived austere lives. They refused to relieve themselves on the Sabbath. My friends, I don't know how you can find the Sabbath a day of rest if you are not permitted to use the restroom. They would take a ritual bath of purification before each meal. And each meal was simple water and bread. They believed that their perfection in the pursuit of purity would so impress God, that God would come down and crush Rome and bring for the blessings of the Messianic Kingdom.

But Jesus ticked off the Essenes. He touched lepers. He spoke with prostitutes. He ate with sinners. He hung out with Gentiles. He ignored purity regulations. He showed us that the kingdom of God will not be realized through withdrawing into a religious subculture. We must have contact with the world. Yes, a contact without contamination. But a contact that transfers the power and love of God to heal and help and transform.

The Methodist church, historically, has been a champion in helping us to understand that the church is to make a positive impact on society. John Wesley inspired his movement to be actively involved in the problems and perplexities of the community. Throughout the 1800s, the Methodists pressed for reforms in labor movement, housing, prisons, public education, sanitation, health.

Methodism was strong in England and by the end of the 18th century, the city of London was so lifted by God's love. Literacy increased and poverty decreased. The rates of illegitimate births plummeted. Crime was radically reduced.

Most Christians today do understand the need to plug into our world and give a cup of cold water in the name of Jesus. Robert Putnman has written a ground breaking book documenting that religious Americans are more likely to give money to a homeless person, return excess change to a shop clerk, donate blood, help a sick neighbor with practical care, spend time with someone who is depressed, offer a seat to a stranger and/or help someone find a job.

Regular church attenders give almost four times as much money to charity as their secular neighbors. Regular church attenders more than double the secular crowd in volunteering to work among the poor, the infirm, or the elderly.

Hollywood can make Christians look like clowns – but we are still the salt of the earth and the light of the world. And to use the words of Hebrews 11 – the world is not worthy of the precious people of God. The way of the kingdom is not a holy retreat where we hide out and disconnect from the issues of the day. But we touch our world with courage and compassion.

As Christians, we do not have a theology of triumphalism. We don't believe that the church will Christianize the world. Our hope is in the Second Coming of Christ. Jesus Christ will return. When He comes He will put down all opposition and set up His blessed reign from Jerusalem.

That blessed hope motivates us to be activated now. We want to give the world a preview of what that millennial reign will be like. We want to manifest the nature of God in His love and benevolence. We want to relieve present pain and give people tangible expressions of God's loving care. We are evangelists and activists because we live in the light of the Second Coming of Jesus Christ.

During World War II, the French had an active underground force. If you could have asked a member of the French underground, "What are you trying to accomplish with your ragged handful of soldiers and your small efforts to be freedom fighters?" they would have said, ""It's obvious! We are trying to defeat the Nazi armies who have been occupying our land." You would have protested, "But you have a small group with few guns and limited weapons. You are up against one of the mightiest military machines in the history of the human race. You don't stand a chance against them." They would have answered, "We are determined to fight to liberate our land because we know that right now just over the English Channel, a military machine is being built with trained soldiers and sophisticated weapons. We know that just over the ocean, in the United States, armies are being assembled and bombs are being built. These forces know where we are and what we are doing. Any day now a signal will be given and a huge invasion force will get on ships and planes and submarines and will come across to join up with us. That invasion force, the English and the Americans, they will link up with what we are doing and carry us to victory."

Our labor is not in vain in the Lord. We are struggling to make a difference in this wicked world and sometimes we get discouraged and overwhelmed, but right now an army is being built in heaven and any day now forces will arrive here from the other side of the Milky Way. John said in Revelation 19:11-16 "Now I saw heaven open a behold a white horse and He that sat on it was called Faithful and True, and in righteousness He judges and make war...the armies in heaven followed Him on the white horse...and He has on His robe and on His thigh a name written: King of Kings and Lord of Lords."

A HOLY COMMUNION CHURCH

I Corinthians 10:14-22

Therefore, my beloved, flee from idolatry. I speak as to wise men; judge for yourselves what I say. The cup of blessing which we bless, is it not the communion of the blood of Christ? The bread which we break, is it not the communion of the body of Christ? For we, though many, are one bread and one body; for we all partake of that one bread. Observe Israel after the flesh: Are not those who eat of the sacrifices partakers of the altar? What am I saying then? That an idol is anything, or what is offered to idols is anything? Rather, that the things which the Gentiles sacrifice they sacrifice to demons and not to God, and I do not want you to have fellowship with demons. You cannot drink the cup of the Lord and the cup of demons; you cannot partake of the Lord's table and of the table of demons. Or do we provoke the Lord to jealousy? Are we stronger than He?

I got behind a SUV on the road and I noticed the bumper sticker., "I am a mother of twins – I nap at red lights." My mother could certainly identify with that kind of fatigue. She knew the strain of raising twin boys. Whether you have twins, triples, singles or no children – we all discover that existing can be exhausting. That's why I love to preach about the Eucharist Meal. Here is a station of refreshment to empower us to persevere in this journey of faith. The sacrament of baptism gets us into the race of faith. The sacrament of the Lord's Supper nourishes and strengthens us to stay in the race.

It is fascinating to observe the formula Jesus established for Holy Communion and how He used that same exact formula to feed the 5,000 in the open field. In the upper room, where He introduced this Sacred Supper, we are told that the distribution of the bread involved four verbs: Took! Bless! Break! Give! He took the bread. He blessed it. He broke it.

He gave it. This is the shape of the Supper. These same four actions were employed when Jesus fed that huge crowd in the desert place. The little boy's lunch was presented to Him. He took the bread. He Blessed it. He broke it. He gave it. The similarity must be intentional.

Jesus fed the 5,000 to illustrate the nature and purpose of Holy Communion. That large crowd on the hillside needed a miracle to survive. They had no food with them and they had no access to a grocery store in that desert place. We are in the wilderness of a world. We cannot sustain ourselves spiritually. But Jesus says, "Come and Dine." When we partake of His table, He fills us and satisfies.

The day following this miracle of multiplying the little lunch, Jesus launched into a wonderful teaching concerning the power and preciousness of participating in Holy Communion. "...Unless you eat the flesh of the Son of Man and drink His blood, you have no life in you. Whoever eats My flesh and drinks My blood has eternal life, and I will raise him up at the last day" (John 6:53-54).

Do we really value and appreciate this blessed gift, Holy Communion? Holy Communion is not just a ceremony so that we can remember a gift—it is a gift. How we view the nature of the Supper will determine its frequency—how often we observe it. The Bible and church history are clear that the primitive church and the early church observed Holy Communion every Sunday. It was considered an essential and integral part of worship. As the vine communicates its vitality and virtues to its branches through that blessed union, so Christ communicates His abundant life with His people as we enjoy communion with Him at the table. Why would we not want this vital connection when we come to worship?

I have heard some say, "Well, Holy Communion is so holy and sacred, we need to guard it and not do it very often. We don't want to get too familiar with it. The more we take Communion, the less meaning it will have." If that is true that frequency creates an unhealthy familiarity, then let us apply that principle to other things too. Prayer is holy, so let's not pray every day. Bible reading is holy, so let's not open the Book too often. Obviously, we want to do something more if it is so holy and meaningful. Since Communion is so holy and sacred—we need to do it more, not less. Jesus said, "As often as you eat this bread and drink this cup." He did not say, "As seldom as you do it." It is important that we understand its value and blessedness. There are six simple words I want to use to help us appreciate and anticipate this amazing sacrament.

The Holy Communion is:

1. A Time for Remembrance

2. A Time of Reverence

3. A Time of Reality

4. A Time of Reconnecting

5. A Time of Rehearsal

6. A Time of Receiving

A Time for Remembrance

"In the same manner He also took the cup after supper, saying, 'This cup is the new covenant in My blood. This do, as often as you drink it, in remembrance of Me.'"– 1 Corinthians 11:25

Too often Christians suffer from amnesia. There are some things we should forget. Paul said, "Forgetting those things that are behind" (Philippians 3:13). Some things we need to forget—past grudges, past grief, past guilt. There are some things we must never forget. Never forget from where He brought us. Remember the pit from where He rescued us. Isaiah 51:1 says, "Look to the rock from which you were hewn, and to the quarry from which you were dug." Holy Communion is to be a central part of our worship to help us to remember that which we must never forget - the death of Christ.

Some of you may remember the tragic death of President Kennedy. I was just turning 2, so I don't remember. But my mother remembers where she was and what she was doing when she got the news. There was great mourning over the death of the President.

On that same day, the same assassin killed Officer Tippett in Dallas but almost everyone has forgotten his name. We remember the death of Kennedy because he was the President of the United States and because deliberate steps have been taken to make sure we don't forget. He was interred at Arlington Cemetery and his family paid for an eternal torch at his grave, a gas light that is to never go out, as a perpetual reminder of his life and death.

Six months after his death, many schools were named after him. Idlewild Airport became John F. Kennedy International Airport. Cape Canaveral became Cape Kennedy. Massive effort were made to guarantee that no one would ever forget that day in American history.

Remembering is not something that is automatic. We choose to remember. Memory is selective—we decide what from the past is worthy of remembering. The entire past is not some golden era to be rehearsed with nostalgia. Rather, we retell those events of the past that really matter.

The most important event of human history is the sacrificial, substitutionary death of Jesus Christ. When we gather together for worship, the center piece of that worship is the Supper—where we do this in remembrance of Him.

A Time of Reverence

Therefore whoever eats this bread or drinks this cup of the Lord in an unworthy manner will be guilty of the body and blood of the Lord. But let a man examine himself, and so let him eat of the bread and drink of the cup." -1 Corinthians 11:27-28

The reading we shared from I Corinthians 11 is so stabbing and severe that it scares some Christians so badly, they never dare take Communion. God was actually killing some church folk because they were mishandling this sacrament. I see many Christians on Sunday who will not receive the bread and wine. I ask them, "Why?" They respond, "I am not worthy. I fussed with my wife last night. I am angry with my neighbor right now. I caved in to five temptations this week. Maybe I will partake next Sunday, if I express a more holy life this coming week." There are many churches that emphasize that Holy Communion is designed for Christians doing well. It's a kind of reward for the victorious. It's a privilege for those believers who are spiritually prepared.

But my friends, if we are sinning and struggling—we need Holy Communion all the more. This is medicine for the soul. The Supper is not a victory banquet for those Christians who have reached some high level of spiritual maturity and perfection, but it is a nourishing meal for those Christians who are hungry and famished and weak.

Notice that Paul did not say you have to be worthy to take Communion. We could never be worthy of this. Paul said we must take Communion in a worthy manner. The church at Corinth took Communion in a very vulgar and carnal manner. Prior to Communion they had what was called the *Love Feast*. But there was no love in the *Love Feast*. It was a big Sunday church picnic. Each family brought their own meal and didn't think about other families present who could not afford a nice slab of barbecue ribs and potato salad. And so there was great inequality at the feast and no one was sharing. There was also too much drinking going on at the feast. So that, when it was time for Communion, some Christians were still physically hungry and some were drunk and some were filled with pride because they had more chicken in their basket than others. It was a mess.

They were defaming this holy sacrament with such a casual, cavalier, self-centered attitude. Paul accused them of having no discernment. They did not have proper respect for the material body of Christ that was nailed to the cross and they did not have love for the mystical body of Christ that was surrounding them.

And so, Holy Communion is a time for reverence. We do exam ourselves. We do confess sins. We even hear the words from scripture, "On the night that Jesus was betrayed He took bread" (I Corinthians 11:23). We recall that Judas was in that upper room, he belonged to the Twelve, and yet he proved to be false. He betrayed Jesus Christ on the night that the Lord's Supper was instituted. All of us are capable of such dark apostasy. We don't come to the table judging others, but we come judging ourselves asking, "Lord is it I?"

But this aspect of self-examination is not to be the prevailing mood of Holy Communion. We confess our sins and then we quickly claim His fresh forgiveness and appropriate His cleansing. For this is why Christ died.

Beloved, the focus of Communion is not our lack of performance, but it is the perfect sacrifice of Jesus Christ. Let us avoid the trap of getting self-absorbed at this holy moment. We remember Christ. Holy Communion is not a dark funeral that carries such weight and gravity. It is a feast. Yes, we must have soberness at the table, but not somberness.

Holy Communion is a sign and seal of the new covenant. Covenant means that Christ is faithful to His promises. He will never leave us nor forsake us. So, in spite of our faults and failures, we come to the table with great joy because Jesus never fails. He is our champion of love.

A Time of Reality

"For my flesh is food indeed, and My blood is drink indeed."
John 6:55

Holy Communion is a sacrament, which means that the Holy Spirit gives us the power to participate in what is being symbolized. Yes, the bread and wine are symbols. But they are not empty symbols. They are sacramental symbols. They are the means by which we participate in the intangible and spiritual realities without which there is no life.

When we pray the prayer of consecration over the elements, we do not believe that prayer changes the essential structure of the bread and wine. The bread is still bread. The wine is still wine. But the prayer of consecration sets apart these common things—bread and wine—sets them apart so that they are assigned to function in a special and holy activity. The Holy Spirit fills the Eucharist Meal and the living presence of Christ fills the meal so that entire event is a mystical experience with Jesus Christ.

The Supper is more than a mental activity where we reenact what Jesus did. But rather, we relax the mind, open the heart and enter into to the present power of the Cross of Christ. Holy Communion is more than Christ with us in an intellectual and symbolic way. Rather, He is with us in a real and supernatural way that transforms our lives. The miracle does not take place in the bread and wine—the miracle takes place in us. We indeed eat His body and drink His blood and we receive His life into us.

Our text is very helpful to us at this point. Paul tells us that pagans go into their idolatrous temples and they actually enter into a fellowship with demons. There is a dark energy in that room. Behind those idols are real evil spirits with whom they have contact. Then he makes a comparison between that pagan ritual and Holy Communion, "You cannot drink the cup of the Lord and the cup of demons" (I Corinthians 10:21). Just as pagan worship connects people with evil spirits, so Holy Communion connects believers with the living Christ.

This is the glory and grace of Holy Communion. Christ gives Himself to us and we enjoy the benefits of Calvary's Cross. The value of Holy Communion is not dependent on our ability to recall all the details of the crucifixion. It is not dependent on our mental imaging of the passions of the Cross. It is not dependent on our recollection of Good Friday. The value of Holy Communion is built on the promise of Christ. He said that when come to His table we are truly eating His body and drinking His blood and thus we live forever.

A Time of Reconnecting

"Therefore, my brethren, when you come together to eat, wait for one another. But if anyone is hungry, let him eat at home, lest you come together for judgment." 1 Corinthians 11:33-34

Paul says that Holy Communion is a time to discern the body of Christ (I Corinthians 11:29). In this context, he meant that it is time to recognize and celebrate the family of God. There are no solitary Christians in the world of salvation. There are no do-it-yourself Christians. There are no self-help Christians. There are no Lone Ranger Christians. Salvation is not a private deal with God. The Eucharist Meal reminds us of that fact.

Even in our homes, the family meal has fallen on hard times. Very few families actually sit down in the evening to enjoy a meal together. When I was growing up, the supper time was so special. We ate early because mom worked a short tour schedule at the phone company. She had to be at work at 6 p.m. So we would eat our meal at 4:30 p.m. I remember it so clearly. It was a daily routine. We kids would get home from school, change our clothes and play outside. Then we would clean up and sit down to watch *The Flintstones* at 4 p.m. This would settle us down and prepare us for the meal. Then at 4:30 we would be called to the table.

Sometimes we would eat goulash, spaghetti saturated with tomato paste, hamburger with mac and cheese, chicken and dumplings, or sometimes it would be ham and green beans. No matter what is was, supper was wonderful. Mom and dad sat at each end of the table. Deb, Jimmy and I in the middle. We discussed the events of the day. It was all about relationships.

That meal represented real sacrifice. Mom made a real investment. She prided herself on preparing "real potatoes". I would watch her peel potatoes. Dad prided himself on rolling out the dough and making homemade apple pie. There was a labor that went into every meal. We had to wash up. We had to get our attitude right. Corn had to be shucked. Green beans snapped. Mom made iced tea herself—southern sweet and oh, so good. The table had to be set. We kids had to wash the dishes—no dishwashers! The sacrifice that was made for the meal to take place represented love. We sacrifice for one another. That's the nature of love.

We are coming to a day where the love of many are waxing cold (Matthew 24:12). Family meals are rare. We now have TV dinners, instant food, frozen dinners and Chinese take-out! Families are scattered at meal time. No conversations are taking place. There is a deconstruction of hospitality in the home. The warmth and intimacy are getting away from us.

In the church, we understand that fellowship is something that is vulnerable and unity is something tenuous. The Lord's Table empowers us to affirm our family identity and sustain and nurture our unity. The Lord's Table celebrates the ultimate Sacrifice of Jesus Christ and it strengthens us to live sacrificial lives so that we can love one another even as Christ has loved us.

A life without sacrifice is an abomination. The table binds us together where the texture of spiritual fellowship is thickened and we are mandated to dine with those whom we may not like and prefer, but it is not my table, it is the Lord's Table. Each one at the table is God's VIP guest, and we are to embrace and honor all of God's children.

A Time of Rehearsal

"For as often as you eat this bread and drink this cup, you proclaim the Lord's death till he comes."
— 1 Corinthians 11:26

The Holy Table points to the past—we remember His death. It points to the present for the risen Christ sits at the table with us. But it also points to the future—for the anticipation of the eternal and glorious feast of God's people in heaven.

Jesus transformed the Jewish Passover into the Lord's Supper. It is fascinating how He did that. Jesus and His disciples were in the upper room celebrating Passover. The four cups of wine were enjoyed with special prayers of thanksgiving that recalled the deliverance of the Jewish people out of the bondage of Egypt. The Lamb and side dishes were eaten in between the drinking of those cups of wine.

Jesus shocked His disciples when He picked up the third glass of wine and recited the special praise assigned to that cup, then He continued with some words that were beyond the script. With that third cup in His hand, He said, "This cup now has new meaning and significance. This cup is the blood of the new covenant. It is my blood poured out for you for the forgiveness of sins. Drink it!" (Matthew 26:28 paraphrased by author).

Then He made the announcement that He was changing the program. He would not drink the fourth cup. He would leave that final cup alone. He said that the third cup would be the last one drunk on that particular Passover celebration. Jesus said, "After this third cup, the cup of my blood, I will not drink again from the fruit of the vine until I drink with you in the kingdom of my Father" (Matthew 26:29 paraphrased by author).

Jesus did not finish the meal. The meal is ongoing. We are eating and drinking today. And there is still one cup in the Supper that is future. The conclusion of the meal is not reached until Jesus drinks that fourth cup with all believers at the Marriage Supper of the Lamb. The Eucharist Meal is a foretaste of our eternal feast in heaven. It is a rehearsal and a promise of the wedding feast that will be consummated when Christ comes for His beloved.

A Time of Receiving

"I am the bread of life." —John 6:48

What is salvation all about? Simply receiving by faith the goodness, grace and gifts of God. That's why Christ instituted Holy Communion. To enforce within our hearts the nature of salvation. What do you do at a table? You recline. You sit. You receive. We have a tendency to turn salvation into some human achievement. We are not in charge of salvation, we can add nothing to it.

Holy Communion forces us into the right posture, we sit as sinners in need of Savior. We see Him not just as a teacher from whom we learn. We see Him not just as an example whom we imitate. We see Him not just as a hero who inspires. There is another focus. We see Him as the Lamb of God who takes away the sins of the world. The Eucharist sets salvation in an ambience of sheer acceptance. Christ gives Himself to us and we receive.

Salvation is not primarily a truth we figure out. It is not primarily an ethical behavior we must carry out. It is not some complicated doctrine we must comprehend. It is not some electric emotion we must experience. Salvation is a meal to eat!

Not everyone can comprehend a doctrine. Not everyone can obey a precept. But everyone can eat a piece of bread and drink a glass of wine. The Eucharist builds a fence around the grace of salvation. Eternal life is not learning something, or performing something. It is eating a meal. We simply believe on the Lord Jesus Christ.

I love the words in the Song of Solomon 2:4, "He brought me into his banqueting room and His banner over me was love." This is social, but it is personal. At the table, Christ sits with you and He shares Himself. He says, "I love you. I want your company. I desire to have intimacy with you. I long for your attention and affection. Here – eat this! I gave My body for you. Here - drink this—I poured out my blood for you. Enjoy. Be forgiven. Be cleansed. Be healed. Be satisfied. Be renewed. I love you. You are mine and I belong to you."

A NEW COVENANT CHURCH

Jeremiah 31:31-34

"...the covenant that I made with their fathers in the day that I took them by the hand to lead them out of the land of Egypt, My covenant which they broke, though I was a husband to them," says the Lord. "But this is the covenant that I will make with the house of Israel after those days," says the Lord: "I will put My law in their minds, and write it on their hearts; and I will be their God, and they shall be My people. No more shall every man teach his neighbor, and every man his brother, saying, 'Know the Lord,' for they all shall know Me, from the least of them to the greatest of them," says the Lord. "For I will forgive their iniquity and their sin I will remember no more."

Happy New Year!

That simple statement should excite all of us because we love new things—new cars, new clothes, new songs. God knows all about our delight in novelty, so He blesses us as the God "who makes all things new" (Revelation 21:15). He knows how to thrill and satisfy us by introducing new experiences into our lives.

The greatest "new thing" He has ever extended toward His people is the "New Covenant." To say we have a New Covenant implies that there was an Old Covenant, and indeed there was. There was a covenant under Moses that God established with the Children of Israel. This was a very specific relationship-contract structured by God to engage Israel in a distinct lifestyle of ceremonial worship, political theocracy, ethical obedience and spiritual reality. It was a relationship outlined by certain benefits, commandments, conditions, expectations, promises, and regulations.

Although the covenant was constructed by God, it was not really robust enough to survive the sinful situation of people, so it served as a temporary covenant until something with more permanence could be implemented.

In the context of our Scripture reading, we find Jeremiah weeping over exiled Israel; the people of God had been condemned to Babylonian captivity due to their repetitive offenses against God's covenant. Despite the pitiful condition of the nation, Jeremiah preached hope to this feeble, failing group of exiles. He prophesied about a New Covenant that God would make with His people—a covenant that would far outweigh and outlast the Mosaic Covenant.

Today we hear advertisers promote their products with the slogan "new and improved," and we LOVE IT! Who wouldn't opt for "new and improved" over "old and inferior"? Unfortunately, the new is not always improved.

Personally, I love Coca-Cola. I don't drink much of it because I try to keep my weight down, but I love it. It truly is "the pause that refreshes." It doesn't matter if I drink it from the fountain or the soda bar, from an aluminum can or a steel can, from a glass bottle or a plastic bottle—the container does not matter, *I LIKE COKE*. However, something disastrous took place in 1985. I don't know what they were thinking, but the chairman of the board of the Coca-Cola Company stepped out on a bold experiment. They altered the formula and came up with a new taste called "New Coke." What? The protest (which I took part in) was so great that in just ten weeks after the introduction of New Coke, the company brought back the old formula and called it "Classic Coke." Now, Coca-Cola fans everywhere can rest easy.

A product that is presented as "new and improved" may in fact be new, but novelty does not always guarantee an improved quality. How can we be sure that this New Covenant between God and His people is better than the old one?

Let's look at a couple of verses found in Hebrews:

> ➤ *"Jesus has become a surety of a better covenant." Hebrews 7:22*

> ➤ *"But now Christ has obtained a more excellent ministry, inasmuch as He is also Mediator of a better covenant which was established on better promises."* *– Hebrews 8:6*

The Word of God gives confirmation that the New Covenant is superior to its predecessor—it is truly new _and_ improved. The New Covenant will not disappoint us. We will never be forced to drag back the Mosaic Covenant and call it "Classic Covenant." No! The New Covenant is the real thing. It is the pause that refreshes our souls.

What is so special about this New Covenant? What new formula does this covenant contain that makes it so much greater than the old? What benefits can it offer that the Old Covenant could not?

The New Covenant Gives Us...

1. A New Clarity
2. A New Simplicity
3. A New Universality
4. A New Spirituality
5. A New Liberty

The New Covenant Gives Us a New Clarity

"For the law, having a shadow of the good things to come and not the very image of the things."– Hebrews 10:1

"So let no one judge you in food or in drink, or regarding a festival or a new moon or Sabbaths, which are a shadow of things to come, but the substance is of Christ." – Colossians 2:16-17

When we see a shadow coming around a corner, we have a rough idea of what is casting the shadow, but sometimes the reality can be quite different. The shadow reveals but also obscures. In the New Covenant, Jesus has emerged from around the corner, and we see Him far more clear. Shadow gives way to sunshine. Prophecy gives way to fulfillment. Type gives way to antitype. Symbols give way to reality. Pictures give way to personality. We see Jesus *face to face.*

The New Covenant enables us to truly behold the glory of God: "For the Word was made flesh and dwelt among us, and we behold His glory, the glory of the only begotten Son of God, full of grace and truth" (John 1:14).

The New Covenant Gives Us a New Simplicity

"Therefore by Him let us continually offer up the sacrifice of praise to God, that is, the fruit of our lips, giving thanks to His name." – Hebrews 13:15

Worship under the Old Covenant was encumbered with countless external elements and wearisome ceremonies—exact procedures, expensive sacrifices, extensive programs, and endless rules. Worship was exhausting! In the New Covenant, the ceremonies of the old find

184

completeness in Christ, for He fulfills the Law. Jesus is the full reality of the old forms and figures.

- The true sacrifice
- The true temple
- The true priest
- The true king
- The true prophet
- The true Passover

When an artist wants to create a painting, he or she will first sketch rough lines. These lines anticipate the more precise and defined strokes of the paintbrush. Once the paint is applied to the canvas, the rough lines have served their purpose and become obsolete; they blend in with the painting and become part of the finished product.

Ceremonial worship of the Old Covenant was a rough sketch of grace; now, we are able to revel in the freedom of simple worship, for the tedious laws have been fulfilled in Christ. Worship is plain, yet profound. In Christ, there are dimensions of glory that will never be discovered, and so we come to church on Sunday morning with a spirit of awe and astonishment. We offer up a sacrifice of praise, give thanks to God, and focus on the only object worthy of worship - Jesus.

The New Covenant Gives Us a New Universality

"At that time you were without Christ, being aliens from the commonwealth of Israel and strangers from the covenants of promise, having no hope and without God in this world. But now in Christ Jesus you who once were far off have been brought near by the blood of Christ. For He Himself is our peace, who has made both one, and has broken down the middle wall of separation." – Ephesians 2:12-14*

Think of times in history when people have been divided. One prime example is during the Cold War. People picked sides because if you were living in Berlin, you were more or less forced. While the Berlin Wall may have been pronounced and divisive, effectively separating the east from the west, that was nothing compared to the wall of hostility that existed between Jews and Gentiles in biblical times. The veil in the Temple was not the only barrier that characterized the Old Covenant. The wall of separation between Jew and Gentile was high and insurmountable. The Old Covenant was narrow in its scope, focusing solely on the descendants of Abraham.

Thankfully, the New Covenant we embrace today has a much broader scope, offering salvation to all nations and ethnic constellations. The new wine has burst out of the old wineskins! The energy of the New Covenant explodes past the confines of Palestinian geography, and now redemptive blessings are enjoyed by every tongue and tribe.

Believers now enjoy an intimate fellowship with God that is not restricted by cultural limitations. "For through Him we both have access by one Spirit to the Father. Now, therefore, you are no longer strangers and foreigners, but fellow citizens with the saints and members of the household of God" (Ephesians 2:18-19).

The New Covenant Gives Us a New Spirituality

"I will put My law in their minds, and write it on their hearts." – Jeremiah 31:33

The New Covenant involves an outpouring of the Holy Spirit, which is both extensive and intensive. It is extensive in the sense that God pours out His Spirit upon all flesh. It is intensive in the sense that He ensures that each one knows Him personally. Furthermore, the indwelling of the Holy Spirit transforms us with impulses to lead a new life and equips us with power to carry out those impulses.

Gatorade marked its 50th anniversary in 2015! Did you know there are now thirty-eight bowl games? I know because I watch college football bowl games. Many of these games are sponsored by Gatorade. Advertisers of Gatorade used to ask the question, "Is it in you?"

For the 50 year anniversary, however, they employed a new slogan - "Win from Within." The commercials featured athletes with marked success—running touchdowns, dunking basketball goals, and hitting home runs. The viewers were told that the reason these athletes win is because they have been fueled with energy from Gatorade. "Win from Within. Is it in you?"

People of the Old Covenant could not succeed morally because the Law was not within them. It was etched on stone, preached from prophets, and scribed on religious law books - but it was not *inside them*. The condition of the heart was still corrupt and selfish. The outward pressure of morality could not make them virtuous. The external Law only made them mean and miserable by labeling them as transgressors.

Thankfully, Jeremiah prophesied that the New Covenant would be different. The Law etched on stone would be etched on hearts. The letter of the Law written in books would become the Spirit of the Law within the soul. New life would be expressed from deep within. Virtue and victory would be produced not by the works of the Law, but by the fruit of the Spirit of God.

Our quest for holiness is not achieved by mere imitation, but through internal habitation. The Holy Spirit dwells within us, and we enjoy intimate union with Christ—a reciprocal indwelling that fuels, energizes, and empowers us. When we face temptations that we cannot overcome, problems we cannot solve, pressures we cannot bear, and challenges we cannot meet - what can we do? We humbly offer a prayer to God reminding Him that the flesh is weak and that He promised that when we are weak, He is strong.

The New Covenant Gives Us a New Liberty

"Our sufficiency is from God, who also made us sufficient as ministers of the new covenant, not of the letter but of the Spirit; for the letter kills, but the Spirit gives life. But if the ministry of death, written and engraved on stones was glorious...how will the ministry of the Spirit not be more glorious? For if the ministry of condemnation had glory, the ministry of righteousness exceeds much more in glory." -II Corinthians 3:5-9

The Old Covenant was characterized by condemnation and death. Its very inauguration was trumpeted by the giving of the Law within the terrifying smoke of Mount Sinai. A Law that sinners could never measure up to! The situation was hopeless. In the New Covenant, we are no longer slaves of the Law. Instead, we are sons and daughters of God! "For you have not received the spirit of bondage again to fear, but you received the Spirit of adoption by whom we cry out, 'Abba, Father.'" (Romans 8:15). God loves His children unconditionally, and the verdict of heaven is one of acceptance and the divine emotion is one of adoration.

Heaven is not for good people! Heaven is not for perfect people! Heaven is not for religious people! Heaven is for people who have been forgiven! The Old Covenant people could not enjoy the full forgiveness of God. The demands of the Law were always weighing heavy upon tender consciences and the sacrificial system of continual offerings were systematically reminding them of their sinful state.

In the New Covenant, we enjoy a judicial forgiveness that is complete, perfect, and eternal. God forgives our sins completely and remembers them no more! We are free to dwell in the abundance, sufficiency, and joy of this covenant of grace. The Lord's Table replaces the altar of sacrifice so that the Eucharist celebrates the finished work of Jesus Christ who offered a perfect and eternal sacrifice for sin.

The Law	Grace
"Do this and live."	"It is done—now live."
"Try to do your best."	"Trust and now rest."
"The best are condemned."	"The worst are justified."
"Pay what you owe."	"Paid in full."
"The wages of sin is death."	"The gift of God is eternal life."
"The soul that sins will surely die."	"Believe on Christ and you shall never perish."
The law was something they had to keep. Grace is something that keeps us.	

Each church should be a *New* Covenant church. Everything must be saturated with grace: the gospel of grace preached, an atmosphere of grace cultivated, and the dispensation of grace shared with the lost.

There is an old *Dennis the Menace* cartoon that wonderfully portrays this grace. Dennis and his little buddy Joey are leaving the home of their kindly neighbor, Mrs. Wilson, cookies in hand. Joey asks Dennis, "I wonder what we did to deserve this?" Dennis then explains, as only a child can - "Look Joey, Mrs. Wilson doesn't give us cookies because we are nice. She gives us cookies because *she* is nice."

Our relationship with God is based on His sovereign grace and our contract with heaven is signed and sealed with the blood of Jesus Christ. In Luke 22:20 Jesus said, "This cup is the new covenant in my blood, which is shed for you." The Eucharist table reminds us of the graciousness of the new covenant. This is "the real thing!" This is "the pause that refreshes!"

A CALVARY GOSPEL CHURCH

John 11:47-57

Then the chief priests and the Pharisees gathered a council and said, "What shall we do? For this Man works many signs. If we let Him alone like this, everyone will believe in Him, and the Romans will come and take away both our place and nation." And one of them, Caiaphas, being high priest that year, said to them, "You know nothing at all, nor do you consider that it is expedient for us that one man should die for the people, and not that the whole nation should perish." Now this he did not say on his own *authority;* but being high priest that year he prophesied that Jesus would die for the nation, and not for that nation only, but also that He would gather together in one the children of God who were scattered abroad. Then, from that day on, they plotted to put Him to death. Therefore Jesus no longer walked openly among the Jews, but went from there into the country near the wilderness, to a city called Ephraim, and there remained with His disciples. And the Passover of the Jews was near, and many went from the country up to Jerusalem before the Passover, to purify themselves. Then they sought Jesus, and spoke among themselves as they stood in the temple, "What do you think—that He will not come to the feast?" Now both the chief priests and the Pharisees had given a command, that if anyone knew where He was, he should report *it,* that they might seize Him.

I get amazed with how good we humans are at manipulating words and cleverly constructing sentences. We are somehow able to hide the truth of reality and only convey what we want to convey. I heard about this wealthy family who hired a man to write a biography of the family. But they were embarrassed to tell him that one member of the family, uncle John, had been convicted of a capital crime and had literally died in the electric chair. The biographer thought for a minute and said, "Oh, that's no problem. I can fix that, you're alright." So when the book came out, here is what he said about John who died in the electric chair, "Uncle John occupied the seat of applied electronics in one of the most prominent institutions of this state. He was bound to that position by the strongest of ties and his death came as a great shock."

We humans have great skill and ingenuity in putting people in the light we want them to be seen in, regardless of the facts. Sometimes we want to put them in a positive light, sometimes in a negative. We have the ability to do that. We have a great ability to put ourselves in a positive and pleasant light, even though our hearts may be evil.

In John 11, the religious leaders of Jerusalem were plotting something terrible. They were hateful and hostile toward Jesus Christ. They were discussing how to get rid of Him, yet they made it appear as if they were doing something noble and wonderful for the nation. They were clearly calculating murder, but they did not want to give the appearance that they were acting as murderers.

They needed a good, religious excuse for justifying their evil deed. Listen to how their reasoning and their discussion developed, "This is the last straw. If He wants to heal the sick up in hinterland, up in the sticks of Galilee, well, let Him do it. But why does He have to come to our parish, in the very suburbs of Jerusalem? And think of it, to raise a man from the dead! That's too much! It's intolerable! What are we ever going to do with a fellow like this who insists on healing the sick and raising the dead in our backyard? Before we know it, everyone is going to believe on Him. That will be a fine kettle of fish. And then the Romans will come and take our place and our nation" (John 11:47-57; paraphrased by author).

This jealous bashing of Jesus Christ evolved into a discussion of the present protection and future preservation of their beloved nation Israel. They suggested that this Jesus movement would eventually lead to the Romans invading Jerusalem with destructive power to crush a religious uprising. The chief priest thought of a good reason to kill Jesus. He thought of a basis by which they could murder Jesus and still save face and look religious. "Isn't Jerusalem the Holy City of God? It is unthinkable that we would be so passive and unconcerned as to do nothing about the preservation of our nation. This Jesus is threatening the future of Israel. It is bad that we would have to put Him to death, but the welfare of the nation is at stake. If His ministry continues and His following gets bigger, Rome will not be happy. Sometimes it is necessary that a man die so that the nation is saved. Isn't that what happens in war? Innocent people die in battle so that the interest of the nation is saved. This is case in point. Jesus must die so that the nation is spared. We must make plans to kill him. We can't feel guilty about it, either Jesus dies or our entire nation will perish."

This high priest, Caiaphas, was a gangster, a rascal, a racketeer. But on that day when he spoke to the religious council, he preached a great gospel message. When he said, "Jesus must die so that we can live" – he was actually prophesying. The High Priest didn't know it when he said it, but he was prophesying. "It is expedient that one man die for the nation. So that the nation does not perish." None other than the High Priest, Caiaphas, clearly articulated what the Bible teaches about the atoning death of Jesus Christ.

We know that Jesus died, but the burning question is this, "Why did He die?" No other question is more vital, crucial and central than this. Why did the Lord Jesus Christ die? What is the relationship between the suffering and death of Jesus and our eternal salvation? How do these two things relate?

Our Place

It is essential and imperative that each of us understand clearly where we are—our place. The Bible tells us that every single one of us, by nature and by choice, are in a very dangerous and desperate situation. We are like a man who is one under the sentence of death for his crime. And if that's not enough, the poor fellow is dying of a fatal disease.

That is the predicament in which every human being finds himself. We are under the just condemnation of a holy and righteous God, and a fatal spiritual malady is destroying our being. We are condemned and dying. Our whole being has been drastically affected by the virus of sin.

The religions of this world will admit that human beings are in trouble, but they do not go far enough in defining the human predicament, thus they offer superficial solutions that don't really address the need. The religions of the world admit that we are drowning, but somehow they have the notion that we can save ourselves. They seek to give us swimming lessons. They throw out a branch and tell us to get a grip. And if that doesn't work, they try to make our descent to the bottom of the ocean more comfortable.

This is in contrast to the message of Jesus Christ. He does not stand on the shore barking out orders that we should swim harder. He does not jump in with us and say, "I'm a fellow struggler just like you. Let's join hands and go to the bottom together." He does not merely point to the shore and leave the rest up to us. Rather, He stands on solid ground, reaches out a strong saving hand, and promises to deliver us from the powerful currents and dangerous waves that would swallow us up in death.

Jesus Came to Take Our Place

So many people really don't understand why Jesus died. Some see His death as an expression of God's willingness to love us and bless us. That the Cross is kind of a plus sign, a symbolic statement that God is on our side. Well, that is true, but it is not sufficient. The Cross of Christ is not just a sign of God's love, but it is the very basis upon which a holy God can forgive, justify and accept a condemned sinner. We need more than a new attitude. For a man who is dying of a fatal disease, he needs more than a warm feeling and happy mentality about God.

Before there can be a right relation, there has to be a real transaction. And that is the meaning of the atoning death of Jesus. It can't be that God is eager to forgive us and the death of Jesus is meant to melt our hardness as we accept His forgiveness. The Cross is not primarily to be a sentimental influence, but it is an actual payment for our sins. A price was paid on that old rugged Cross—something real happened there. A transaction was made. Heavenly business was being taken care of. Something significant took place that was essential if you and I are to live spiritually and eternally.

God told our first parents that if they disobeyed they would surely die. That threat was fully carried out in the dying of our Lord. "My God, My God, why have Your forsaken Me" (Psalms 22:1 The Bible is clear. In I Tim 2:6 Paul states, "Jesus gave His life a ransom for all." "All we like sheep have gone astray; we have turned, every one, to his own way; and the Lord has laid on Him the iniquity of us all" (Isaiah 53:6).

There was a transaction. Something amazing was accomplished and achieved. His death was substitutionary. He was our substitute, bearing our eternal judgment. I Peter 2:24 says, "He bore my sins in His own body on the tree." In II Corinthians 5:21 we read, "He who knew no sin was made sin for us." I Peter 3:18 says "He suffered once for sins, the just for the unjust, that He might bring us to God."

Someone asked James Denny, "What is the meaning of Christ's death?" And that great theologian said, "Bearing shame and scoffing rude, in my place condemned He stood. Sealed my pardon with his blood, hallelujah, what a Savior." Or to use a more contemporary song, "I was guilty with nothing to say. They were coming to take me away. Then a voice from heaven was heard that said, 'let him go and take Me instead.' I should have been crucified. I should have suffered and died. I should have hung on that cross in disgrace, but Jesus, God's Son, took my place."

We Take Jesus' Place

If we have seen our place, and how Jesus came to take our place, it's not complete until we see this grand and marvelous truth—we take Jesus' place.

The man said in giving his testimony, "You know what Jesus has done for me? He swapped with me. He took my sin, I take his righteousness."

This is a blessed exchange!

He took our place of misery and shame so we could be lifted and exalted to eternally share in His place - a permanent dweller in the Father's house. He offers to us His place. John 17:24 says, "Father I will that they, also whom thou hast given me, be with me where I am, that they may behold My glory." This prayer of Jesus expresses strong desire. "Father, I deeply desire. I strongly and desperately want. Father, I determine that those whom thou hast given me will be with me." I can't comprehend this. He has promised to be with us even to the end of the age. But He's interested in more than the short span of our lives. He wants His people to spend eternity with Him. Where is He? At the right hand of the Father. In the Glory! He wants us to be with Him.

I am a sinful speck of dust and would consider it an extraordinary concession of divine grace to just enter through the gate of heaven. If I even made it over the threshold and was given permission to stand on the edge of this celestial society, that's far more than I could ever expect. But He's not satisfied with that. Jesus Christ wants me with Him.

"The pleasure of your company is requested at..." Wouldn't you like to get an invitation of that sort? That anyone would consider my company a pleasure is a delightful thought to me. But when the living Christ says, "I want Timothy with me," isn't it amazing? To realize that He's not just aware of my existence, but He has an interest in the fellowship that I can give to Him. He wants me to dine with Him forever. Not just for a little interval of time. He does not want us to be with him on a rotating basis so that we each get ten minutes with Him every one million years. No! We will be with Him where He is throughout all of eternity.

"Father, I will that they also whom thou hast given be with me where I am, that they behold my glory" (John 17:24). Someday, all of us saved sinners are going to stand on the sea of glass and sing the song of redemption. We will gaze upon His glory. These frail, trembling hands of flesh will grasp the crown of life. These feeble knees shall kneel before the celestial throne and cry "holy, holy, holy." These feet of clay will walk the street of gold in the city of God. These poor stammering, stuttering tongues shall join the mighty chorus and sing "Worthy is the Lamb." These eyes shall behold His glory.

How can it be? How can this amazing prospect ever take place? He took my place, so I can take His place.

The high priest was trying to justify a murder. He was trying to cover up a hideous crime, but in searching out a logical reasonable and believable excuse, he stumbled upon a wonderful spiritual gospel truth. "It is expedient that Jesus die. It is profitable and beneficial that He die. If He dies, the nation will not perish."

If Jesus Christ is your personal savior, you will not perish.

ABOUT THE AUTHOR

Dr. Timothy Wood began to preach at the age of ten. Throughout his teenage years he preached in local churches around the Baltimore, Maryland region. At the age of 16 he moved to Cleveland, Tennessee to study Bible at Lee University. A year later he was licensed to preach with the Church of God denomination. He continued his schooling at the University of North Alabama where he earned a Bachelor's degree in Education and a Master's Degree in Education. He pursued his education with Logos College, Jacksonville, Florida where he earned his Master of Divinity degree. He earned his Doctorate degree in Christian Education from Faith Theological Seminary in Tampa, Florida. He has served as Evangelist, Associate Pastor, Senior Pastor, Christian Education Director, Elementary School Principal, High School Teacher, and College Professor of Biblical Studies. Presently, he is serving in Waldorf, Maryland as Senior Pastor of Calvary Gospel Church and President of Calvary Christian College.

www.ingramcontent.com/pod-product-compliance
Lightning Source LLC
LaVergne TN
LVHW051233080426
835513LV00016B/1553